Walking with Nobby

CONVERSATIONS WITH NORMAN O. BROWN

by Dale Pendell

MERCURY HOUSE — SAN FRANCISCO

MERCURY HOUSE IS A NONPROFIT PRESS
GUIDED BY A DEDICATION TO LITERARY VALUES
AND THE FREE EXCHANGE OF THOUGHT

All rights reserved. No part of this book may be reproduced in any form or by any electronic or mechanical means without permission in writing from the publisher, except by a reviewer or critic who may quote brief passages in a review

Thanks to Thomas N. Brown and the Brown estate for permission to publish "Love Hath Reason, Reason None," and to Clayton Eshleman to republish "From Politics to Metapolitics," which first appeared in *Caterpillar*. Selections from *Apocalypse and/or Metamorphosis* and *Love's Body* used by permission of
The University of California Press

©2008 Mercury House
www.mercuryhouse.org
Proofread by Kelly Burch
Printed by Versa Press

Library of Congress Cataloguing in Publication Data on file.

Walking with Nobby

CONVERSATIONS WITH NORMAN O. BROWN

For the Dionysian Principle—

    that gives us hope, if neither solace nor rest.

Abbreviations to works
of Norman O. Brown
cited in the text:

HT	*Hermes the Thief*
LAD	*Life Against Death*
LB	*Love's Body*
FPTM	"From Politics to Metapolitics"
CT	*Closing Time*
A/M	*Apocalypse and/or Metamorphosis*
LHR	"Love hath Reason, Reason None"

•

(*FW* refers to *Finnegans Wake,* by James Joyce)

•

Norman O. Brown commonly referred to himself as "NOB" (pronounced "N. O. B."). In this book I omit the periods.

Walking With Nobby

v   *Abbreviations*
viii *Biography*
xi *Preface*

2   *Fall Creek, June 1993*   NOB's house; chance; NOB's palinode; the Coyote Principle; God's poisonous mushroom; reincarnation & Buddhism; DP's story of a funeral; chance/divination/luck; random killings; LSD & the unconscious; Hitler as a problem; occultism; *Love's Body* too Christian; John Cage, chance, & poetry; DP talks about squirrels; Nietzsche & compassion; the responsibility of writers; Dionysus & Apollo.

39 *Pogonip, January 1994*   The Oneida community; complex marriage; the Savior as the clitoris; politics; Antinomianism; Elaine Pagels & Christianity's irredeemable flaw; Robert Graves & Laura Riding; the Grateful Dead; "make love, not war"; the Sixties; mass psychology & fascism; sheep & goats; tragedy & farce; puns & false etymology; Christianity; marriage, love, & affairs; M. C. Richards; NOB's conventional life; DP's Jungian tendencies; NOB & the arcanum.

81 *Wilder Ranch, July 1995*   Camille Paglia; DP meets a Marxist-Freudian; censorship; Aristos/Demos; the State; King Lear; *Love's Body* too Christian; alcohol; a herd of cattle; *Hermes the Thief*; Cabeza de Vaca; fathers & mothers; Oedipal dreams; Justice; Chance; Reincarnation & Buddhism; Christ/Dionysus; Justice/Geometry; Pascal; money as shit; wild pigs; Artemis & "what *really* happened"; Dionysus/Shiva; a naked girl; Mormonism; the goddess naked; *Pharmako/Poeia* & literal metaphors; mothers; mother's bedroom; Milton & the Bible.

A Trail Guide

143 *Sunset Beach, January 1996*   DP on drugs; death; the *pharmakon* & Serres' parasite; Freud & cocaine; Marx, Blake, Camille Paglia & "the canon"; *sobria ebrietas* & ecstasy; the War of Poisons; Maxwell's Demon; wagers; Daniel Dennett; Wendy Brown; "Nature"; Spinoza; hemlock; Jacques Derrida; the "Soul" & Buddhism; DP's scourge.

175 *Fall Creek, March 1997*   Marriage; Oedipus & the vagina; women; Christ/Dionysus; Ariadne; Nietzsche; love/chance; Blake; NOB's lost book; the language of poetry; Dionysus & Coyote; love; DP's wasted life; mistakes & wagers; Nothing; Epilog.

Appendices:
201   "From Politics to Metapolitics," Brown, 1967
215   "Love Hath Reason, Reason None," Brown, 1993
225   "The Gray Lovers," Pendell, 1991
226   Bibliography
229   About the Author

NORMAN O. BROWN, 1913—2002

Norman O. Brown, scholar, philosopher, and poet, was a fearless intellectual of exceptional integrity, ready to follow the implications of his ideas wherever they might lead. His methodology was one of exploration rather than an explication or rationalization of a preconceived premise. His axioms were minimal and traditional, rooted in the classics, in myth, and in poetry. He wasn't afraid to admit his mistakes; to the end of his life his concern was to get it right, that his efforts and legacy would not shame him as he joined the immortals.

Popularly, he is perhaps best known for a few of his more quotable and radical aphorisms, such as

> *Freedom is poetry, taking liberties with words, breaking the rules of normal speech, violating common sense. Freedom is violence.*

or

> *I am what is mine. Personality is the original personal property.*

or

> *The money complex is the demonic, and the demonic is God's ape; the money complex is therefore the heir to and substitute for the religious complex, an attempt to find God in things.*

Brown was born 1913 in El Oro, Mexico, 10,000 feet above sea level. His father, Norman Charles Brown, was a mining engineer, Anglo-Irish-Protestant from Donaghmore, County Tyrone, Northern Ireland. His mother (whom his father met on a ship on his way to Mexico) was Cuban-Alsatian, "with the beautiful, exotic name of Margarita Maria Catalina Coloma Deschwendt." In 1921 Brown's father moved the family first to Ireland, and then to England, so that his children could have a British education. Brown excelled in school, usually ranking at the top of his classes, as well as being captain of the rugby team, and won scholarships. He earned his BA and MA at Balliol College, Oxford, where his philosophy tutor was Isaiah Berlin. After graduation, Brown

BIOGRAPHY

emigrated to the United States to earn his Ph.D., in Classics, at the University of Wisconsin, under A. D. Winspear. Brown believed (proudly) that he had triple citizenship: Mexican, British, and American.

During World War II, Brown worked for the OSS, the Office of Strategic Services (along with Carl Schorske and Herbert Marcuse) trying to understand fascism. After the war he obtained a position at Weslyan University. His first book, *Hermes the Thief*, is an investigation of why the god of thieves and trickery became the god of commerce, a study which led him to Hesiod's *Theogony*, which he translated.

After the defeat of Progressive Henry Wallace (for whom Brown had worked) in the 1948 presidential campaign, Brown became disillusioned with electoral politics and sought a deeper understanding of historical and cultural processes. To this end he began an exhaustive study of Freud, culminating in *Life Against Death: the Psychoanalytic Meaning of History* (1959), which won him international recognition. In 1966, while teaching at the University of Rochester, Brown published *Love's Body*, a continuation and refinement of his ideas in a poetic style. Brown himself considered *Love's Body* to be his definitive work.

In 1968 he came to the newly created University of California, Santa Cruz, where he was named Professor of Humanities in recognition of the breadth of his studies. While at Santa Cruz Brown published *Closing Time* (1973), a study of James Joyce and Giambattista Vico, and *Apocalypse and/or Metamorphosis* (1991), his final collection of essays. During this period Brown also published in several of the leading poetry and literary magazines.

In the last decade of his life, in which these conversations occurred, he had become interested in the idea of chance, and how it might help solve what he perceived as problems in *Love's Body* and his attempt to formulate a Dionysian Christianity.

PREFACE

The most valuable standpoints are always the last to be found, but the most valuable standpoints are always the methods. —Nietzsche

My first walk with Norman O. Brown was in the early 1980s. After a hiatus from formal schooling of fifteen years, I had enrolled in the University of California at Santa Cruz to complete my undergraduate studies, and, at the encouragement of Lynn Sukenick, was taking Brown's class on mythology. In addition to his stature as a world-class intellectual, Brown was also a great teacher, confrontative in a direct and personal way that caught many students off guard, either baffled or, in my case, outraged. The final straw was a quote from Vico's *New Science*:

Poetic truth is metaphysical truth, and physical truth which is not in conformity with it should be considered false.

I wrote the professor an acerbic letter, parodying some of his lines, and Professor Brown, evidently amused by my emotional response, suggested a walk. On that short walk (which was just crossing the campus on the trails through the redwoods), I was told:

1. that I bore an attitude of amused contempt;
2. that my writing was contemplative and not active;
3. that my criticisms were merely the most common feelings on the campus and not useful in the least; and
4. that I would never see the goddess naked.

It was only the last barb that got me. Goddesses were an object of study and interest for me, and seeing them naked, I believed, something like a birthright for a poet. The old fox had not only outraged my intellect, but insulted my destiny.

I responded with a letter and a poem, and that led to further walks. Nobby liked my poetry, but we argued about everything else. After my graduation, we kept in touch only by occasional letters, until, in 1993, prompted by my friend Tom Marshall and several of Nobby's ex-students living in Mexico, I reestablished personal contact. Tom was taking regular walks with Nobby, and suggested that I do the same. I wrote to Nobby, then called him, and we set a date for the next week.

Nobby had retired from active teaching at this time, and he walked almost every afternoon (except for weekends, which were reserved for family). If he didn't have company, he walked alone. Nobby followed a routine, and adhered to it strictly. He worked in the morning until twelve, when his wife Beth served lunch. Then he napped, then out to walk at one. Nobby was a strong walker, even in his eighties when he used a cane, and we often covered three or four miles. The walks were punctuated by stops and starts, brief rests on logs or on the ground, and frequent laughter. We both carried index cards with us, and each of us would occasionally pen down a phrase, a reference, or an idea.

Sometimes on our early walks I tried to show off by quoting lines or stanzas from poems that I knew by heart. At such times, Nobby would merely purse his lips and nod, or grunt and say "That's good." It was only later that he began to recite quotations himself—usually long passages from the classics, and as often as not in Greek.[1]

---

[1] Nobby's repertoire went far beyond the passages he had learned as a student, and included poems and passages from his current studies. Memorization, for the most part, is no longer considered to be either essential to, or even a part of, learning. That is, no one thinks that by "merely" memorizing something that one "understands" it. (One thinks of Julien Sorel). On the other hand, how deep could anyone's understanding be, if that person doesn't know the relevant passage "by heart?" In Zen koan practice, every case must be memorized (some of them are lengthy). The student must first be able to recite the case back to the teacher before presenting his "understanding" of it.

These walks span several years—during that time Nobby and I met sometimes weekly, weather permitting, sometimes monthly, sometimes less frequently. The format was fairly constant: meet at one o'clock at Nobby's house, drive to one of a half dozen favored trailheads, and then walk for several hours. Then home by five, because he ate at six. This last rule was seldom violated, and was evidently an issue of domestic contention if it were.

The basic "deal," at the beginning at least, was that Nobby wanted to learn about plants, a subject I knew well. In return, Nobby offered "The Western Tradition." Nobby once told me, "You should have known me when I had teeth." Well, that's a terrifying thought, because Nobby loved to attack, and hitting below the belt was all too often his preferred mode. After I got my bearings I came to expect personal attacks, accepted them, sometimes was able to make a few digs of my own, and finally we had one of those special understandings where one can say *anything*. No hold was barred, and no subject taboo, and baiting was an expected part of the dialogue.

My purpose here is not to present any summary or explication of Brown's philosophy.[2] Rather, hopefully, in some of our exchanges, I can offer a glimpse into the methods of mythopoetic thought. And perhaps some hint of the wit, sarcasm, and heart of the ferociously irreverent man behind the philosophy.

As Nobby's walks were always personal, this has to be my story as well as his.

---

[2] The first full-length philosophical study of Brown's work, *The Resurrection of the Body,* by David Greenham, appeared while this book was being prepared for press, and is recommended for those philosophically inclined. The book somewhat emphasizes the early Brown, though it runs through to *Closing Time.*

FALL CREEK, JUNE 1993

Professor Norman O. Brown and his wife Beth lived in Pasatiempo, a gated community built around a golf course a couple of miles above Santa Cruz. There was a guard at the gate but I never stopped and the guard always waved. The Brown residence was up above the far end of the golf course, a California ranch style house nicely landscaped in front and back, surrounded by chaparral.

Nobby answered the door and then excused himself to get into his walking shoes. Beth said hello and we exchanged pleasantries until Nobby returned. Nobby asked me where I'd like to go. I said I didn't know, where did he have in mind? Nobby said "let's go to Fall Creek." I said fine and we decided to go in my car. Nobby retrieved his automatic gate opener out of his car, so that we could use the back entrance. Nobby knew the shortest way to Felton, and directed me, advising me which lanes were best to be in at the different stoplights. We were in Felton in five minutes.

The Fall Creek Trail is a loop walk of about three miles with splits in the trail on both the outbound and inbound legs,

NOTES

[1] This was NOT what I was expecting. It was as if in the eight years since I had last seen Nobby we had exchanged our roles. At our last meeting Nobby had been the one chiding me about my scientific attitude. Since then I had been heading for the NOB of divine madness, the 1967 NOB, and here was the 1993 NOB seemingly headed toward what I considered the most non-magical of reductions.

[2] I had no idea what he was talking about. Maybe Nobby wasn't sure himself. Later that year Nobby wrote:

> The idea of chance, so much identified with John Cage; my friend since 1960; but I would not listen. I was a determinist; first a Marxist determinist; then Freudian determinist. The world of chance; the world of chance mutations. In Love's Body, Ch. XII, it says "Nothing happens for the first time." That is dead wrong: everything happens for the first time. That is the meaning of chance; it contradicts both the Christian idea of eternity and the Nietzschean idea of eternal recurrence. (LHR, see Appendix 2)

Nobby was uneasy with this piece. On the title page of the typescript it says "NOT TO BE CITED. IN PROCESS OF REVISION." Early in 1995 Nobby discussed the paper by telephone with Jay Cantor. Jay followed up their conversation with a letter:

> The chance universe leads you then to a new sense of non-recurring time. Mutations occur often, or often enough, so that recurrence is unlikely, and newness is likely indeed. But I don't think this requires you to say that everything happens for the first time.
>
> I think this leads to an epistemological problem, in any case. Language—and knowledge—depends on recurrence ...

In May of 1995 I wrote to Nobby and added a third layer: "*I disagree with Jay: think that chance does indeed require everything to be happening for the first time. All the time. (And in each repetition!)*"

On the other hand, am I the only one who thinks that "recurrence" is being taken too literally? What about, as I've heard people say, "And then with my next girlfriend, the exact same thing happened...."? Like that. Nobby may have been thinking of Heraclitus: fire/newness/Dionysus. Snow also has a way of making "all things new."

2   Fall Creek

resulting in four possible permutations—of which we only ever used three. Mostly it is an easy, flat trail through the redwoods, though on one route there are several short steep climbs where we would use our hands to grasp shrubs or outcropping boulders. The trail crosses the stream several times.

The understory is typical coast redwood forest—trillium, violets, wild ginger, elk clover, blackberry and thimbleberry. Ivy and periwinkle are rampant, despite occasional attempts by the park rangers at control.

We were able to park the car within a quarter mile of the trailhead. We both grabbed light jackets to take along—somewhere the sun was shining, but not in a redwood forest. With his hat and cane, Nobby looked rather jaunty.

Nobby started by asking about my family, then again inquired about my job. Feeling rather virtuous, I told him that after having lived most of my life as a street poet (mountain variety), having a regular job in corporate America was developing my character. Nobby laughed derisively, "How schoolboy. Haven't you gotten over that yet?" We were off.

NOB: I am looking at chance. I think that life is an accident.[1]

DP: Welcome to the twentieth century.

NOB: The old NOB, of *Love's Body*, where I differed from Cage—I now think that NOB was wrong and that John Cage was right.[2]

DP: So are you going to recant?

3 Nobby turned to take in the effect of his words on me, his chin elevated with that air of superiority he would assume when he felt he had scored a strong point. He wasn't disappointed. I had been working hard to temper my scientific skepticism, in order to swim more freely in mythopoesis, and here was Mr. Mythopoesis defending the Philistines. I had started in physics: "science" seemed like the old news. Nobby told Tom Marshall that if he were starting today, he would study biology.

4 The rise of fundamentalism in the ensuing decade and a half has made me reconsider "the greater danger."

5 That is, even the "chance mutations," the basis of Brown's newness, are chance by definition; that is, axiomatically.

> *The hypothesis of chance is precisely what a hypothesis is devised to save us from. Chance, in fact, = no hypothesis. Yet so hypnotic, at this moment in history, was the influence of the idols and of the special mode of thought which had begotten them, that only a few—and their voices soon died away—were troubled by the fact that the impressive vocabulary of technological investigation was actually being used to denote its breakdown; as though, because it is something we can do with ourselves in the water, drowning should be included as one of the different ways of swimming.* (Owen Barfield, Saving the Appearances, 64)

When "Chance" is used as an explanatory principle, in effect replacing "Providence," the word might more properly be capitalized.

NOB: I must write a palinode. We must embrace science.[3]

DP: But doesn't science already have the upper hand? Isn't the greater danger scientific reductionism? That self-satisfied smugness that Gurdjieff called "nothing-butism"?[4]

NOB: No, we must go forward, with science!

DP: Hasn't science become the new religion, with chance as the new god?[5]

NOB: Then we agree that it is theology.

DP: I agree that chance has become the *deus ex machina*. But it could be that there is no such thing as chance—that there are no accidents.

NOB: That's teleology.

DP: Why? I'm not saying that there is a plan, or a director, just that everything follows laws.

[6] The conversation was moving quickly and a great deal was being left on the table, unresolved. The equation Dionysus = chaos I accepted as a definition. That chaos doesn't follow laws is more problematical. Just because *we* can't determine what will happen, the system can still be said to be deterministic; there is no need to invoke God or chance or free will as a causative agent. In any complex system of interacting bodies, the cumulative effects of an error in the measurement of the initial conditions, no matter how small, will inevitably result in unpredictable (chaotic) behavior.

Democritus allowed chance (αυτοματια) in cosmic events (say ... the origin of the universe) but left earthly and human actions determined by atomistic mechanics. Epicurus added chance deviation (παρέγκλισις), but while the "swerve" may sidestep determinism, it's orthogonal to the question of free will, which still needs a mind-body coupling.

In physics, such attempts began within a year of Heisenberg's publication of the Uncertainty Principle in 1927, none very successful. More recently, Roger Penrose (*Shadows of the Mind*, 1994) has suggested that the ability of a quantum system to get information from "null measurements" could provide the necessary non-computational basis for consciousness. For our discussion, it is enough to know that the quantum state vector, Ψ, which is the solution to the Schrödinger wave equation, is a complex number that, strictly, has no physical analog—and that it is all the information we have. The *square* of the state vector, Ψ^2, does have physical meaning: it is the probability of the event in question occurring. The mind/body coupling, at this point, is still a pun: parapsychologists use "psi" to refer to the information and energy transfer necessary for telepathy ("psi-gamma") and psychokinesis ("psi-kappa").

David Greenham points out that in Hesiod's *Theogony*, Chaos (Χάος), which Brown translates as Void, comes first:

> *This is not the place of creation itself but the place where creation will take place when Earth and Sky come into being. (It is also the place, or gap, that ... we will come to know as the imagination).* (Greenham, *The Resurrection of the Body*) >>

NOB: That's why we need chance: it lets in Dionysus, chaos. The Lord's Prayer is all wrong: "Our Father, who art in heaven" is not Dionysian.[6]

DP: (I had many thoughts, but I wanted to follow Nobby to Heaven.) What about "Thy will be done"?[7]

>> [7] Cf. "John Cage," a lecture by Norman O. Brown at Wesleyan University, December 22-27, 1988, at the symposium held in honor of Cage's seventy-fifth birthday:

> *We live in historical time: the process is history*
> *we submit to the yoke of historical necessity*
> *It is by reason of this fact that we are made perfect by what happens to us*
> *rather than by what we do*
> *(Meister Eckhart quoted in* Silence*)*
> *We suffer history*

The full Meister Eckhart quote, as given in *Silence* (p.64) is:

> *But one must achieve this unselfconsciousness by means of transformed knowledge. This ignorance does not come from lack of knowledge but rather it is from knowledge that one may achieve this ignorance. Then we shall be informed by the divine unconsciousness and in that our ignorance will be ennobled and adorned with supernatural knowledge. It is by reason of this fact that we are made perfect by what happens to us rather than by what we do.*

Cf. Dōgen:

> *When the Self advances to confirm the ten thousand things, that is delusion. When the ten thousand things advance and confirm the Self, that is realization. (Dōgen, Genjōkōan)*

And lastly:

> *We slip out from under the reality-principle, into the truth; when the control breaks down. By great good fortune, gratis, by grace; and not by our own work or will. (LB 244)*

⁸ I was thinking of surrender, as in Sufism, and in the sense implicit in zazen, or by extension, "accepting what comes." Nobby meant that if there is a higher power orchestrating everything, as in predestination, there is no chance. Of course, if the higher power has a chancy nature, both statements are true.

⁹ Nobby didn't mind contradicting himself. Cf.

> "What orthodox psychoanalysis has in fact done is to reintroduce the soul-body dualism in its own new lingo, by hypostatizing the "ego" into a substantial essence which by means of "defense mechanisms" continues to do battle against the "id." (*LAD* 158-159)

¹⁰ A corollary of the Coyote Principle is that One World Government, the great hope of Einstein and other utopians, is a bad idea. And imagine nuclear bombs and nuclear power plants with Coyote at the controls—and he always gets there, eventually.

Likewise, drug laws will never keep Coyote off of drugs. Wouldn't it be better to just accept that Coyote is going to take drugs, let him buy them at the drugstore, and deal with it as best as possible at the neighborhood level? The alternative encourages Coyote to take the control of prisons, police departments, drug cartels, street gangs, and any public office with possibilities of corruption.

NOB: That denies chance.

DP: That permits chance![8]

NOB: You're too Christian, it effaces the ego.[9]

DP: In formal systems there is no reveling. The closest they come is the Monte Carlo method: that lets in chance. Formal systems are grammatical, wild systems have what I call the Coyote Principle.

NOB: What's that?

DP: That no matter how well things are planned out, Coyote will find a way to fuck it up.

NOB: (Laughing) How comforting. Well then, the struggle is over, there is nothing that we have to do.[10]

(We walked on until we came to a fork. Nobby directed us up the "high" trail—a steep climb on a slant up the hillside. He asked me what I was working on and I told him about Pharmako/Poeia, *my book about psychoactive plants.)*

NOB: How are you going to handle it?

DP: Poison.

NOB: Good! Venus, venom, venerate. See H.D., *Tribute to Freud.*

(I pulled a card out of my pocket and jotted down the lines. Nobby seemed pleased. As we were passing under some oaks, I spotted the pale yellow cap of an Amanita phalloides.*)*

DP: Ahhh, speaking of poison, look at this.

NOB: Is that poisonous?

DP: (That was my cue. I spoke slowly and solemnly and stretched it out.) This is so poisonous that people have died from only a few bites. It destroys your liver, but it's a slow death. You don't begin to feel any symptoms until the mushroom is all digested and it's too late. In fact, they say that the longer it is before the onset of symptoms, the less chance there is of survival. Then it's

[11] Cf.

> The whole problem is to break with the doctrine of univocation. For if we believe that the Old Testament has only one meaning, it is certain that the Messiah has not yet come. In Protestant literalism there are of course prophecies in the Old Testament: but these are literal prophecies: what Luther called sensus propheticus literalis. The crux is univocation versus reincarnation: the Psalms may refer either to David or Christ, but not both. (LB 202)

vomiting and diarrhea and extreme pain for two days. Feces red, skin yellow. At that point some people seem to recover. All the symptoms vanish and they are often discharged from the hospital. That is the last fatal sign. A few hours later all the symptoms return and the person dies in great agony.

NOB: This mushroom does that?

DP: Yep. Some say you should wash your hands merely after handling it.

(Nobby seemed suitably impressed and we resumed our walk.)

NOB: Why did God put that poison here?

DP: (Very satisfied) I'm shocked that you ask that. To help us to our next life.

(Nobby smiled and started asking questions about my personal life, what my routines were, how I spent my time. Sometimes he repeated questions that he had just asked, as if my answers made no sense or impression. Sometimes it seemed like he wanted to label me: "Ah, so you are one of the blah-blahs." He knew I didn't like it and that probably encouraged him. Partly, I think, he was trying to form a mental picture of me that would fit into the categories of his system, but in another way he was challenging me to state my position with enough precision to avoid clichés. I had to tell him about my Zen practice.)

NOB: (Derisively) Buddhism! So you follow some ... guru?

DP: (Thinking, "What a nasty man this is") I have a teacher, yes.

NOB: I'm bothered by the reincarnation in Buddhism. It dulls the maw of death. It takes away the alienation.[11]

(I argued that such a view of reincarnation was folk Buddhism, that rebirth in the Six Worlds was happening all the time, in this life, but it didn't get me off the hook. I glanced

12 I stashed that one away as future ammunition. Nobby surely sensed the tension between his statement and Freud's "disturbing the sleep of humanity."

13 That is, "mere" chance—that there is no message from the gods. In Homer, the lots were shaken up in Hector's helmet to eliminate human bias, so that the will of the gods might be known. "Chance" was not involved.

14 I might add that as we already have several good words for meaningful coincidence, such as auspice and omen, "synchronicity" was never part of the discussion. There are several problems with synchronicity. First, with its five syllables, synchronicity sounds like it is an actual physical theory or principle that explains something—it's not: it's not a theory and it doesn't explain anything. The allusions to physics in Jung's essay are nonsense—Pauli told him as much. The allusions fail even as metaphor. The use (misuse) of physical concepts in mystical contexts has become common, "quantum" mostly being introduced by those who wouldn't know how to calculate a trajectory. However, as careless as "New Age" literature is in using snippets of physics to explain "paranormal" phenomena, the post-structuralists are even worse, particularly the French. (See *Fashionable Nonsense, Postmodern Intellectuals' Abuse of Science*, by Alan Sokal and Jean Bricmont.) At least in the New Age literature it is usually possible to read the text as poetry (albeit bad poetry).

over at Nobby and I could see his own alienation, his individualistic side. He was still a kid in rebellion. Somehow the talk shifted to death, and then to funerals, which Nobby scoffed at. I told him about the funeral of my stepson, who had died in a snowboarding accident two years earlier at the age of twenty-two. I told Nobby how people got up and told the most amazing stories, mostly new to us his parents, or sang songs or left little offerings in his casket. Nobby listened to the story of the funeral closely and questioned me about every detail of the form of the funeral and what kinds of things people said, and how people acted, about the bikers and about my wife's reactions. I suggested that funerals are for the living, to look at it that way.)

NOB: Yes, I would not want to be the one to dissuade others of belief in an afterlife.[12]

(We walked on in silence. I was thinking of my parents' reaction to my own atheism. My father, who was a Methodist minister, wrathfully quoting the millstone passage: "better that a millstone be wrapped around your neck and you be cast into the sea and drowned than that you cause any of the little believers to stumble." And my mother, imploring me tearfully: "You must never never use your wonderful gifts to lead others astray."

We emerged onto a wide part of the trail, where it ran along the stream, so we could walk side by side. I had picked up a branch so that I had something to balance Nobby's sometimes gesticulating cane. The conversation returned to chance.)

DP: Doesn't chance deny the auspices?

NOB: Good question.[13]

(The conversation continued around chance for some time. We talked about chance as denial of God's Plan, and how chance operations were used in divination, and how that implied that the operations were not chance at all.)[14]

DP: I prefer luck to chance.

[15] As in Jaime de Angulo:

> *Without power you cannot do anything out of the ordinary. With power you can do anything. This power is the same thing as luck. The primitive conception of luck is not at all the same as ours. For us luck is fortuitousness. For them, it is the highest expression of the energy back of life. Hence the sacred character of all forms of gambling in primitive life.* (de Angulo: "The Background of the Religious Feeling in a Primitive Tribe")

There is a capriciousness to the shaman's power ally, his helping spirit. That is, you can change your luck by courting an ally, or by ritual propriety (as in Confucius), but, ultimately, it remains a chancy business. The helping spirit may have something else to do just at the moment you most need it.

Cf. Empedocles: "Thus by chance all beings have thought."

"Chance" is usually linked to probability and statistics, and to some form of the normal (Gaussian) distribution (the "bell curve"):

$$y = \frac{1}{\sqrt{2\pi}} e^{\frac{-x^2}{2}}$$

first published by Abraham de Moivre in *The Doctrine of Chance* (1738).

Nobby agreed to read the de Angulo essay. He told me later that he "distrusted" de Angulo, objecting to a footnote where de Angulo calls for the Kuksu myth to be investigated by "real scientists."

[16] Linguistically, this would connect luck to power.

[17] Chance denies meaning to coincidence when it is asserted as literal truth.

> *It would be better to follow the myths about the gods than to be a slave to the determinism (heimarmene) of the physicists. For you can hope to appease the gods with worship, but you cannot appease necessity.* (Epicurus: *Letter to Menoecus*)

Barfield notes that Pope Urban VIII told Galileo that he could teach Copernicanism as a hypothesis opposed to the Ptolemaic hypothesis, but "not as being the truth": >>

NOB: How do you see that?

DP: Chance is statistical, luck has to do with the whims of the gods and with personal power.[15]

NOB: Force, *fortis*. Fortuna is from *fors*, chance, or luck.

DP: And *fortis* also?[16]

NOB: Perhaps.

(We walked on for awhile. Nobby didn't like my "luck" thesis, but he didn't have a ready counter, so he tried a personal attack.)

NOB: So what do you do, play the shaman, take out your tarot cards at one in the morning to impress your dinner guests?

(To this I had no answer. Nobby actually had scored a direct hit, so I just kept walking. Being able to keep walking is one of the particular niceties permitted by the peripatetic method.)

DP: Isn't even "Providence" or "God's Will" better than nihilism?[17]

NOB: I'm not sure of that.[18]

>> *It was not simply a new theory of the nature of the celestial movements that was feared, but a new theory of the nature of theory; namely, that, if a hypothesis saves all the appearances, it is identical with truth.* (Barfield, Saving the Appearances, 50)

I had already tricked Nobby into saying that he didn't want to dissuade people out of their belief in eternity.

[18] However, cf.

> *Literalism makes the world of abstract materialism; of dead matter; of the human body as dead matter.... Literal meanings are spirits solidified into matter; animae become trees, like Daphne; or stone maidens, Caryatids.* (LB 223)

19 I sensed a contradiction. Aristotle distinguished *tyche*, coincidental occurrences in the human world, from *automatia*, chance events in the natural world, the difference being that humans had free will. Still.

20 I was hesitant to mention LSD, knowing that it was grounds for summary dismissal—but there it was. (Besides, I had Francis Crick and Richard Feynman on my side.)

21 Oh, really! Cf. Anaïs Nin:

> [LSD's] *value is in being a shortcut to the unconscious, so that one enters the realm of intuition unhampered, pure as it is in children, of direct emotional reaction to nature, to other human beings. In a sense it is the return to the spontaneity and freshness of childhood vision which makes every child able to paint and sing....*
>
> I did not realize that America with its pragmatic culture had no access to this inner world; it was blocked both by Puritanism and by materialism. (Anaïs Nin, *The Diary, Vol. 6*)

22 Certain aspects of the Kantian manifold, generally hidden or ignored, become sensorily palpable, a link between hallucination, imagination, and "symbolism," all tending to make the metaphorical (if reified) nature of "objective reality" more apparent. (This does *not* mean that you can fly.)

23 That is, within his system. Camus did a little better. With God dead, and absurdity the only truth, what is our ethical foundation? NOB certainly could not be accused of intellectual timidity.

Still, how is Hitler a counter to the random killer? If the random killer is proclaiming the new gospel of chance, what gospel is proclaimed by genocide?

DP: Actually, I'm not either. But let's look at the random killer as a worshipper of chance.

NOB: There are no random acts. Freud.[19]

DP: Okay, Driven into a corner by nihilism and meaninglessness, or, else, that all of his actions are determined by the unconscious, the killer seeks freedom and meaning, confirmation, from Chance. So he makes Chance an offering with his rifle, the chance sacrifice. Writes CHANCE in big letters: RANDOM, the new god.

NOB: Why must the struggle out of existential nihilism be senseless violence?

DP: I don't know, but that's where it took me. I was saved from that state by a life-changing experience with LSD. LSD is the antidote for existentialism.[20]

NOB: Your generation, you all abandoned the intellectual question.

DP: We said that trying to solve it with intellect alone, with disembodied intellect, was part of the problem.

NOB: But you accept drugs? How do you know it isn't all a hallucination?

DP: (Thinking) We could say that dreams are hallucination, would you say that dreams have no meaning?

NOB: No, I can't do that ... But I don't think the killer is chance, I think the killer is the unconscious. Your generation avoids the unconscious.[21]

DP: Maybe the LSD is relevant to that, I'm not sure.[22]

NOB: I will counter your random killer with Hitler. I cannot come up with any argument against Hitler.[23]

June 1993

24 "Backed away" ... to the aegis of poetry, where even the most radical ideas have at least the solace of metaphorical company.

Howard Norman writes:

> The Swampy Cree have a conceptual term which I've heard used to describe the thinking of a porcupine as he backs into a rock crevice: Usá puyew usu wapiw ("He goes backward, looks forward"). The porcupine consciously goes backward in order to speculate safely on the future, allowing him to look out at his enemy or just the new day. (Howard A. Norman, *The Wishing Bone Cycle*)

Ursula Le Guin quotes this passage in her essay "A Non-Euclidean View of California," where she is exploring possible literary forms for utopian thought. In a "hot" society where technology is driving rapid change, the Grand Inquisitor offers a choice of freedom without happiness, or happiness without freedom:

> Perhaps we would do well to find a rock crevice and go backward. In order to find our roots, perhaps we should look for them where roots are usually found. (Le Guin, in *Dancing at the Edge of the World*)

25 "But [Brown's] works will continue to be read by those who are looking for an escape, if not from the human condition as such, at least from the intellectual traditions that have so long dominated our understanding of it: Cartesian rationalism, Lockean liberalism, and the whole tradition of the Enlightenment." (Christopher Lasch, introduction to *Life Against Death*, second edition)

Lasch claims that in calling the distinction between self and not-self "the big lie"—one of Nobby's more Buddhist insights—Brown is siding with Thanatos, not Eros.

26 Herbert Marcuse ("Love Mystified: A Critique of Norman O. Brown") also thought that *Love's Body* was too Christian, and listed eight references to the New Testament as proof. But what really bothered Marcuse was Brown's challenge to the "reality principle," to literal history and to "The Struggle." The good Marxist materialist was both baffled and offended that Brown concluded *Love's Body* with "Nothing." Interpreting Nirvana as extinction, >>

Fall Creek

DP: But Hitler was rational, he had a system. And he worshipped the machine.

NOB: I don't think that solves it.

DP: True. And there are the occult connections.

NOB: Yes, I have Trevor-Roper on Hitler's private papers, and George Mosse.

DP: *Occult Roots of Nazism*. A magical Blavatskian cosmic history wedded to local soil and fatherland. That's why the secular humanist skeptics are so zealous in rooting out unscientific superstitions.

NOB: So you want the shaman. I distrust the shaman, he pretends to be rational. I had all that rhetoric and fake intelligence in *Life Against Death*, and I could have become a shaman after *Life Against Death*—I got lots of letters—but I backed away into *Love's Body*.[24]

DP: I'm bothered by Lasch's foreword to the second edition of *Life Against Death*.

NOB: How's that?

DP: He says that while your methodology is now considered outdated, nonetheless the book is still worth reading. That is to say, "Mr. Kurtz, your methods are unsound."[25]

NOB: I never read it. I'm more concerned with the problems in *Love's Body*. It's too Christian![26]

>> the usual misunderstanding presented in a "World Religions 1A" class, Marcuse found "liberation in Nirvana" anathema.

Greenham examines the diverging paths of Brown and Marcuse in detail, concluding that ultimately it is Marcuse who sides with Thanatos and Brown with Eros. (Greenham, *The Resurrection of the Body*)

27 Enter Article of Faith #1: playfulness is good.

> *Poetry is the solvent which dissolves*
> > *the rigourous stereotypes of political ideology*
> > *the numb automatism of political reflexes*
> > *the somnambulist gravity of literal believers*
> *Theses are the obstructions to be dissolved*
> > *to be loosened up —*
> *Poetry is the transforming spirit of play*
> > *metaphorical play*
> (FPTM, 213)

Or: "Even if nothing else today has any future, our *laughter* may yet have a future." (Nietzsche: *Beyond Good and Evil*)

28 Joan Retallack calls Cage "the Zen-minded composer." I've never understood the association of his chance operations with Zen. There is a great deal more Buddhism hiding in Brown than in Cage.

29 Still a matter of bitterness and contention among Cage disciples. See *Aufgabe* #5: "Re and Not Re 'John Cage.'" In his address, "John Cage," at a symposium at Wesleyan honoring John Cage's seventy-fifth birthday in 1988, Brown characterized Cage's use of chance operations as "Apollonian":

> *Chance operations are an Apollonian procedure*
> *a perfectly sober procedure*
> *the Apollonian "I" remains in control*
> *"I ask the questions"*

and

> *Chance operations avoid real uncertainty*
> *the negative capability of being in uncertainties, mysteries,*
> *doubts, and darkness*
> *The results of chance operations are always impeccable: the*
> *experiment cannot fail*
> *no choice   no error   no blame*
> *I'd rather be wrong*

Brown was so intent on making his point that even Cage's "sunny disposition" was enough to place him with the Apollonians. For Brown to criticize anyone other than himself >>

DP: The playfulness of the mythopoetic method is proof that it can't be all wrong.[27]

NOB: You have to look at Cage, John Cage, and chance.[28]

DP: Cage's chance is so boring—dice! But look, Cage used chance to get the auspices, therefore he conceived the world of auspices as larger or more essential than the realm of chance.

NOB: It's not really clear just how John Cage worked. He wasn't interested in Dionysus—I spoke to him twice about it.[29]

\>> for an Apollonian lifestyle is transparently silly. Nonetheless, Cage was deeply hurt and stated in interviews that Brown had pulled away from their friendship. The reverse seems more true, as Cage mentions in an interview with Joan Retallack (*Aufgabe #5*, 139) that he had received an invitation from Nobby and Beth to visit, and that he hadn't answered.

Jed Rasula (*Aufgabe #5*, 147) sums it up best:

> The two of them, Cage and Brown, stand revealed in the end (furtively, implicitly: shown, not theorized) as those bickering siblings, Shem and Shaun, round whom so much of the mayhem of Finnegans Wake *revolves, which both men would surely consent to having the last word:*
>
>> We are once amore as babes awondering in a wold made fresh where with the hen in the storyabot we start from scratch.
>>
>> So the truce, the old truce and nattonbuff the truce, boys.
>>
>> Drouth is stronger than faction.
>
> (James Joyce, Finnegans Wake, 336)

Brown invokes "To Greet the Return of the Gods" twice in this talk, underscoring, I would say, the unfinished nature of the conversation. <to p.22>

\>\> <from p.21> Brown's "Apollonian" characterization of Cage's music has a reflection in Leonard Bernstein's rebuttal to Theodor Adorno's *The Philosophy of Modern Music*. Adorno, championing the high culture of Arnold Shoenberg, attacks Igor Stravinsky as, among other things, a trickster. Bernstein never uses the terms Apollonian or Dionysian, but clearly Stravinsky the trickster, sampling the music of the proles, is the Dionysian, while the "serious" formalism that Adorno admired and called the true art, Schoenberg's dodecaphonic method, must be the Apollonian. (See Leonard Bernstein, *The Unanswered Question, Six Talks at Harvard*.)

30 How? Several thoughts come to mind:

> *The idea of chance breaks the Christian synthesis and opens up the Dionysian future. Chance disunites; loosens the fabric of the world; introduces an irrational swerve.* (LHR 217)

> *Broken flesh, broken mind, broken speech. Truth, a broken body: fragments, or aphorisms; as opposed to systematic form or methods.* (LB 188)

Or (as just another example) the poetry in the homonymic resonance between two etymologically unrelated words.

31 If chance denies the gods, it denies where the gods live, i.e., poetry.

DP: (Petulant) It proves he had SOME brains in his head. Cage demystified art, but mystified the artist. Like Duchamp.

NOB: You think so? I don't agree.

(The trail narrowed where it climbed the hillside around a large redwood and we moved into single file, Nobby in front.)

NOB: Cage tried to learn from Joyce, but didn't; nor did he learn it from Pound.

DP: Cage used chance to let the Tao in, to let in the environment.

NOB: Cage showed that all is chance, therefore all is poetry.[30]

DP: Or all is science.[31]

(A wooden bridge crossed the stream. We stopped in the middle, leaned on the railing for awhile, and watched the water. We seemed to agree that chance was anti-Christian, that it denied teleology and divine justice. Nobby even admitted that chance was probably too big to be penned up in mathematics. I THINK we pretty much agreed that "not determinism, not nihilism," was what we were looking for. I didn't mention that it was a Buddhist doctrine, but Nobby probably knew, which may be why he kept trying to embrace nihilism, connecting through Dionysus.)

NOB: I was helped in seeing the Christianity of *Love's Body* by rereading Nietzsche. Dionysus versus Christ. *The New Nietzsche* brought me back to that.

[32] I was thinking of ecstasy versus enstasy (through ritual/formality), and Orphism as a salvationist religion, and a stepping stone to Christianity.

> *the wild freedom of the dance,* extasy
> *silent solitary illumination,* enstasy
> (Gary Snyder, "What You Should Know to Be a Poet," *Regarding Wave*)

> *Apollonian Orphism is the preparation for the revolution completed by Dionysian Orphism.* (J. J. Bachofen: *Motherright*: An Analytic Summary Prepared by Norman O. Brown with the Assistance of Sanford L. Segal)

> *The split between Dionysus and Apollo here functions inside another, more profound, split that Orphism made its own: between woman and man, between the impure bestiality of one and the pure spirituality promised the other. Orphism exiles the savage violence of Dionysus into the animal world of woman, who is thus, by her very nature, excluded from the Orphic rule.* (Marcel Detienne, *Dionysos Slain,* 92)

See also Arthur Evans, *The God of Ecstasy, Sex-Roles and the Madness of Dionysos,* pp.145-173.

[33] (Sharpening the tension as part of NOB's methodology.) "The most valuable standpoints are always the last to be found, but the most valuable standpoints are the methods." (Nietzsche—a favorite NOB quote)

[34] A typical NOB pronouncement. Who, after all, does know death? When Brown had talked about the importance of death at the John Cage Festival at Stanford in January 1992, and then turned to look at Cage, Cage looked back at him and said "Nobby, I'm ready." Cage died later that year.

DP: Isn't it Dionysus versus Orpheus?[32]

NOB: We live in a Christian country. Making it "Dionysus versus Christ" sharpens the tension.

DP: (Says nothing, but makes a mental note about "the methods.")[33]

NOB: The will to power part of Nietzsche is too masculine. I think Nietzsche lost the track, he missed the feminine.

(We started walking again. There was a great deal more to pursue here, but I was woefully unprepared, and the thread petered out. I told Nobby my friend Susan Suntree's story of the musical exchanges between Mickey Hart and John Cage. Then I spotted a Scoliopus off the trail. The flower is exquisitely beautiful: an extremely pale lavender mottled with brown. The nodding seed pods are usually bitten off by some animal.)

DP: Look!

NOB: What is that?

DP: It's called "Fetid Adder's Tongue." Look at the flower.

NOB: (Looks) It's lovely.

DP: I've always thought that this is the flower at the end of Rilke's "Parable of Death."

NOB: Cage didn't know death.[34]

[35] Literal definitions of *duende* are "ghost," and "the ability to attract others through magnetism and charm."

> *This "mysterious power which everyone senses and no philosopher explains" is, in sum, the spirit of the earth, the same duende that scorched the heart of Nietzsche, who searched in vain for its external forms on the Rialto Bridge and in the music of Bizet, without knowing that the duende he was pursuing had leaped straight from the Greek mysteries to the dancers of Cádiz or the beheaded, Dionysian scream of Silverio's siguiriya.* (Federico García Lorca, "Play and Theory of the Duende")

("Siguiriya" is a form of deep song; Silverio an Italian-born cantaor of Seville.)

[36] "The bishop travels by express." (Nimzovitch)

[37] Antipodal: chance as nihilism.

DP: Is that duende?[35]

NOB: Yes. So he didn't know love.[36]

DP: Nobby, so from one direction, chance is the essence of poetry, but from the standpoint of "there is only poetry," chance is antipodal.[37]

NOB: The antinomy of "there is only poetry" is truth and science.

DP: That's disgusting.

(My emotional reaction gave him great pleasure. We walked silently after that for ten or twenty yards, Nobby holding his chin up again to show that he had scored. We talked some about the plants—I told a long story about annual and perennial grasses in California—how the annuals had pushed out the perennials—that Nobby liked a lot. I pointed out various wildflowers, reeling off their botanical names. Nobby especially liked Cynoglossum grande, "Giant Hound's Tongue.")

NOB: Look at how much Greek you know!

DP: (I felt full of myself enough to go on the offensive.) I don't think there is too much Christianity in *Love's Body*, I think there is too much Freud.

[38] Susan Sontag, in *Against Interpretation*, characterizes Brown's project as correcting the mistakes of Nietzsche and Freud. Brown broke with Freud by attacking two of his core assumptions: the mind/body dualism, and the "self-evident" value of self-consciousness. Part of Freud's mind/body dualism is seeing sexuality as "lower," and sublimation (art, science, culture) as higher. Breaking with Freud's "primacy of the intellect" implied dethroning the "reality principle" (which sounds like madness ... who could take such a project seriously?).

Brown insisted that self-consciousness must be participatory, Dionysian; that merely remembering traumatic events, as in psychotherapy, was not enough. (Look at the popularity of "seminars," where the audience is invited to consume spiritual truths—even in Buddhism, those sects emphasizing seminars and expositions by enlightened teachers are far more popular than those involving practice.)

Freud accepted the inevitability of culture as it is, thus most "psychotherapy" is concerned with "adjustment," completely ignoring the radical truth that adjustment to a sick, neurotic culture is even more neurotic than maladjustment. So many personal growth workshops (as also the new megachurches) focus on overcoming shame and guilt—that the participants might enjoy the material rewards of a ruthlessly acquisitive culture without pangs of conscience.

Brown grounded his categories in the body. In addition to the more familiar eschatologies of transcendence (Biblical, enlightenment, progressivism, the theories of Marx and Hegel), there is an eschatology of immanence, as in Nietzsche. Sontag points out that Brown based his Dionysian affirmation not in Nietzsche, but in Christian eschatology, with its resurrection of the *corporeal* body. Brown's break with Nietzsche is in rejecting social domination as the price for the fulfillment of the few.

> The highest praise one can give to Brown's book is that, apart from its all-important attempt to penetrate and further the insights of Freud, it is the first major attempt to formulate an eschatology of immanence in the seventy years since Nietzsche. (Susan Sontag, *Against Interpretation*) >>

NOB: Freud was a way for me to get back to the body.[38]

DP: I think the clinical diction in *Love's Body* mars the poetry.

(Nobby didn't look concerned, and the thread was not pursued any further. We were on the return loop of the trail by this time, on the other side of the stream where the trail was narrow and forced us to walk single file. In this situation the person in front, in this instance myself, would occasionally stop and turn around to mark or emphasize a particular point. Alternately, rough sections of trail tended to bring about separation and silence.)

NOB: What is there in Buddhism that you can hook the drugs onto?

DP: Good question. Maybe Dionysus is a bodhisattva. He uses skillful means to awaken those who come close to him. He poisons poison with poison, so that the people recognize community.[39]

NOB: Nietzsche couldn't accept community, for him it was solitary individualism.[40]

>> [39] I elaborate these thoughts in "Amrta: The Neuropharmacology of Nirvana," published by Clayton Eshleman in *Sulfur* #41, and reprinted by Andrew Schelling in *The Wisdom Anthology of North American Buddhist Poetry*. See also "Splitting the Hair: A Dialogue on the Great World Systems," in *Pharmako/Gnosis, Plant Teachers and the Poison Path*.

[40] "The anarchist dream of the noble individual." (NOB, "John Cage," in *Aufgabe* #5) A common misunderstanding of anarchism, which to the contrary, is based on cooperation and "mutual aid." Another line from the same essay is closer to the mark: "The Apollonian discomfort with the crowd."

[41] Tom Marshall notes: "This was his biggest theme with me, not community but species versus person. One thing this concept helped do was to allow the individual's mistakes as part of the species' living."

[42] Biological altruism generally involves "levels of selection": that a certain trait, while not benefiting the individual, may benefit kin or group. R. L. Trivers, also at UCSC, explored the evolutionary consequences of "reciprocal altruism": altruistic behavior directed outside of the group, or even the species.

I was worried that Nobby was headed toward popular accounts that seemed determined to "explain away" altruism (human, or intentional altruism) as a biological equivalent of economic "self-interest." A great deal of effort seems to be expended trying to prove that compassion is *not* part of human nature—the way that Adam Smith is misrepresented as an apology for sociopathic acquisitiveness.

[43] That is, what distinguishes *homo sapiens* from all other animals, the divine spark if you will, is repression: the flight from separation and the inability to accept death:

> *Repression generates the instinctual compulsion to change the internal nature of man and the external world in which he lives, thus giving man a history and subordinating the life of the individual to the historical quest of the species.* (*LAD* 105)

Therefore, from the psychoanalytic point of view, "sociability is sickness."

> *One of the hallmarks of the neurotic personality is a lifelong fixation to the infantile pattern of dependence on other people.* (*LAD* 109)

As if any of us could live without depending on others—human and non-human—not only those living, but the countless generations of those whose work, love, and sacrifice has made our life even possible!

On page 49 of *Life Against Death,* noting the masochistic component of Christian Agape, Brown quotes Augustine: "Love slays what we have been that we may be what we were not."

DP: How do you relate that to chance?

NOB: You have to look at the group, the species, not the individual.[41]

DP: (Silence.)[42]

NOB: You have to look at Empedocles, strife. Empedocles said that all was love and strife.

DP: That brings us to Darwin, natural selection and sexual selection.

NOB: Yes, good.

(I was proud of that one and more conversation followed on Darwin. I had observed that squirrels create for themselves an artificial selective gradient for agility because of their "squirrelish" attitude: that is, they wait until the last split second to jump for safety. I suggested that the particularly human attitude of caring for the unfit created a need for large brains.)

DP: So our salient attitude was compassion, and that required intelligence.

NOB: I think it's masochistic love.[43]

DP: What is it about Freudians, that everything they name stinks of pathology.

[44] NOB himself could be shockingly insensitive—to the point of callousness—not only to his students but even to his children.

[45] I was resisting the image of "tough-minded" opposed to "bleeding heart," that you've got to put your feelings aside and exterminate the unfit—that it's really for the Good.

Still, even if it is compassion that is our most biologically distinctive quality (as I think it is), it is not yet clear that it might not be maladaptive. A large brain has other, more Faustian, side effects, such as intelligence, in the technical sense—the effects of which are, at present, rather dicey.

The fact, however, remains: a child is being beaten (and a horse is being beaten).

[46] In "Dionysus in 1990," Brown posits excess and "wasteful expenditure" as a path to a Dionysian future. (See *A/M* 179-200, and Pendell, *Inspired Madness: The Gifts of Burning Man*, 2006)

[47] Blake, of course: "The road of excess leads to the palace of wisdom." Also:

> *Freedom is fertility; a proliferation of images, in excess. The seed must be sown wastefully, extravagantly. Too much, or not enough; over-determination is determination made into chance; chance and determination reconciled. Too much meaning is meaning and absurdity reconciled.* (LB 248-249)

[48] See my whole *Pharmako* trilogy, especially *Pharmako/Gnosis: Plant Teachers and the Poison Path*.

[49] I was thinking of true Dionysian intoxication as *sobria ebriatas*, as in Philo and Antonio Escohotado, distinguished from vulgar intoxication, for one, by how you feel the next morning.

[50] Similarly, in *LHR*, Brown doubts that "oceanic feelings" are enough to face death.

NOB: (Unfazed) Nietzsche said that pity is the great stumbling block, that which keeps one from becoming great.[44]

DP: (Feeling very threatened) I don't think pity is the same thing as compassion.

NOB: (Slightly bothered by this lame denial) Okay. *Mitleib!*

DP: (I tried whatever lame defenses I could come up with.)[45]

NOB: Nietzsche means beyond good and evil. No ethics. I preached it before but I couldn't accept it. What I'm bothered by is all the wastage.[46]

DP: Doesn't wastage imply teleology?

NOB: I have to think about that.

DP: (Satisfied)

(We walked on, picking our way along the stream.)

DP: What do you think about excess? Tell me something about excess.

NOB: I was about to ask you. Enthusiasm is always excessive.[47]

DP: Maybe what I'm trying to do is to reconcile the "Way of Zen" with the "Poison Path"—the "Way of Dreams" or the "Way of Excess."[48]

NOB: Dionysus is the road of excess. You can't have the potion without the poison.

DP: Dionysus is ivy, which is a protection against drunkenness.[49]

NOB: Do you mean that excess is like a raft that takes you across a river, that then you abandon it on the other side? I doubt that excess is enough to face death.[50]

[51] "The *New Science* is return to divination:

> '*This Science must therefore be a rational civil theology of divine providence.*'" (Vico, quoted in *CT* 67)

Also: "The study of physiognomy shd. be encouraged." (Ezra Pound)

[52] Thus, Pendell: *The Language of Birds: Some Notes on Chance and Divination*, Three Hands Press, 2007 (first published in *Cabinet* #19, 2005).

(The conversation drifted back to my book. Nobby wanted to know about the structure and how far along it was, and how much time I spent writing every day.)

NOB: Your task is to reconcile chance with "return to divination."[51]

DP: Yes.[52]

NOB: How much of the book will be encyclopedic, and how much idiosyncratic? *Krasis*: mix. *Idio*: self. See "idiot."

DP: Half and half. "Mixed."

NOB: You have to slay the minotaur.

(This shut me up. Sensing my surrender, Nobby changed hats to "good cop.")

NOB: (Patting my shoulder) Congratulations, you're going to be an author.

DP: Yes. Rather frightening.

NOB: You may die any day. This book may be your last chance. Do you fear the gods or the judgment of posterity?

DP: The gods—posterity I'm comfortable with.

NOB: Why do you fear the gods?

DP: I'm worried that I've committed a transgression, that it could lead people astray.

NOB: When you publish, you don't know if it's going to be a force for good or a force for evil, there's no telling.

DP: But I feel responsible.

NOB: No, you are not responsible for your work being misunderstood.

DP: Of course I would be responsible.

[53] I remain deeply thankful for this dictum.

[54] Plato, *Republic*.

NOB: No. You can never get all of the mistakes out of it. At some point you have to let it go.[53]

DP: But what about those who publish lies, are they not evil?

NOB: (Turning, with a grin) They're called poets.[54]

DP: (Silence. It was a direct hit. What could I say?)

NOB: (Very satisfied) You can't bring your moralism on a walk with me.

(The trail widened again to a dirt road, bounded by tall oaks and madrone trees. We came to a steel gate marking the end of the trail, not far from where we'd begun.

We had reached the end of the hike. We got into my car and drove through Scott's Valley back to Pasatiempo and Nobby's house. I tried a summing up when we were in his driveway.)

DP: So Dionysus is chance, and chance means science.

NOB: Yes.

DP: But science is Apollo. We have a problem.

NOB: (Smiling) Work on that.

POGONIP, JANUARY 1994

(Nobby was ready to go when I arrived: he had his light tan jacket, his hat, and his cane. He stuck some blank cards into his shirt pocket and handed me the book that I had lent him: Special Love, Special Sex: An Oneida Community Diary, *by Robert S. Fogarty.)*

NOB: This is a bad book.

DP: Why?

NOB: It doesn't describe what their sexual habits were, how it all worked.

DP: It tells about the young men being coupled with older women, and the young women being coupled with older men. And their general attitude toward possessiveness.

1 Without personal attacks, how could we have any fun?

John Humphrey Noyes founded the utopian Oneida community in 1848. Fogarty's thinly veiled moral outrage is as much directed against the concept of arranged marriage as against Oneida's sexual customs—that a couple who were in love with each other were not allowed to marry. One thinks of *The Late George Apley*, by John P. Marquand. A more sympathetic treatment of Oneida, and John Noyes, is in Kenneth Rexroth's *Communalism: From Its Origins to the Twentieth Century*.

Oneida was against possessiveness.

2 The tiny watercolor is at Petworth House, Sussex, where it seems a little out of place among all the gaudy and oversized portraits.

NOB: The community part is too much Father Noyes. But YOU probably think that if we had communities like that everything would be fine.[1]

DP: My generation had Stephen Gaskin and the Farm. They experimented with four-way marriages.

NOB: Your generation liked gurus.

DP: True, but it's not fair to apply that in this case. Gaskin had the integrity to back out of the guru role.

NOB: They had four-way marriages?

DP: Yes, but I think they gradually abandoned them.

(Nobby was VERY interested in the four-way marriages, but I had little more to add. All of this was before we were out of the driveway. I had a book of Blake's paintings stashed in the car, waiting.)

DP: Oh, I found out that for Blake the Savior is the clitoris.

NOB: (Satisfyingly flustered) What? How?

(I showed him a reproduction of Blake's painting "The Last Judgment.")

DP: Bit like mum, wouldn't you agree?[2]

(Nobby looked at the painting a long time and just grunted. I put the car in gear.)

DP: Where shall we go?

NOB: Have you ever been to Pogonip?

DP: No, let's go there.

(Pogonip is a 640 acre hilly greenbelt stretching from the UCSC campus down to the San Lorenzo River. Sloping meadows alternate with copses of oak and madrone. A citizen's committee, "Save Pogonip," started a campaign in the 1970s to save the land from commercial development by the S. H. Cowell Foundation. Gary Snyder contributed a poem titled "Front Lines," sold as a print by Tom Killion.

[3] A major NOB theme, and the main thrust of *Love's Body*. The continuing growth of fundamentalist and evangelical Christianity in no way negates Brown's thesis: the mega-churches, even with their apocalyptic eschatology, are more likely to preach that material success is pleasing to the Lord than to even hint at ecstatic rapture.

[4] Stirpiculture: the breeding of special stocks or races. Kenneth Rexroth points out that the idea of eugenics had broad intellectual support in the late nineteenth and early twentieth centuries. At Oneida, much of the support for eugenics came from the young people returning from college.

[5] In his response to Herbert Marcuse's "Love Mystified" Brown stated:

> *The next generation needs to be told that the real fight is not the political fight, but to put an end to politics. From politics to metapolitics.*

Commenting on this, in an interview with Daniel Charles, John Cage remarked:

> *J. C.: Politics consists of affirming and wanting domination. Norman O. Brown has admirably grasped that the present problem is not political. The problem is to put an end to politics. That is also my opinion.*
>
> *D. C.: So, in the polemic which opposed Herbert Marcuse to Norman O. Brown on this subject, you would place yourself on Brown's side?*
>
> *J. C.: Without even the slightest hesitation. I consider* Love's Body *a great book. Norman O. Brown completely rejects politics, Marcuse fights for it.* (Cage, *For the Birds*)

However, using Hannah Arendt's definition of politics as the speaking of opinion in public spaces, and the maintenance of such public spaces, Brown remained political, as his last book, *A/M*, makes abundantly clear (even as does *Love's Body*). Earthly politics are a reflection of the war in heaven, theomachy: "One emperor on earth, one God in heaven." <to p.44>

Pogonip is only a mile and a half from the Brown residence in Pasatiempo, as the crow flies, but a six mile drive down through Santa Cruz, up High Street, and through the campus. From the hills of the campus Monterey Bay stretches a hundred and eighty degrees in a wide arc, blue and beautiful. There were a few students walking around the campus and Nobby said "The kids are back." Winter quarter was beginning.

The discussion of polygamy and polyandry led us to the occult roots of Mormonism, and a book by John L. Brooke called The Refiner's Fire. *By the time we reached the trailhead the talk had turned to Nobby's recent visit with his friend Carl Schorske at Inverness. Brown and Schorske had been in the OSS together during the war. One of Nobby's students, Barry Katz, had written a book titled* Foreign Intelligence, *about the "Chairborne Division" of the OSS. Their charter was to try to understand fascism. Another member of the team was Herbert Marcuse. As we got out of the car the discussion returned to Oneida.)*

> NOB: The failure of Oneida is the failure of Christianity to provide a framework for Pentecostal, Dionysian phenomena.[3]
>
> DP: Don't you think that the problem with the Oneida community was the move from Dionysian complex marriage to Apollonian stirpiculture? They moved from plural marriage based on desire to centrally planned eugenics. Same mistake as Lenin.[4]
>
> NOB: Carl Schorske and I worked the Wallace campaign. It was after the campaign that I began to seriously question Marx, that there was something wrong with Marxism. I haven't worked in politics since.[5]

(We had been following a trail, but soon left it, Nobby leading the way across the open hillside. Last year's grass was dry and flattened, and the new grass was poking through, three or four inches high. We walked side by side.)

> NOB: Schorske has been reading a book with the thesis that after Milton there could be no epic in English, but the author was afraid of 1968.

>> <from p.42> Nobby was *always* political, even if he was fighting in the halls of Olympus rather than Washington.

The last entry in *Love's Body* is a quote from Lama Govinda's *Foundations of Tibetan Mysticism*:

> *Thus the body of the Enlightened One becomes luminous in appearance, convincing and inspiring by its mere presence, while every word and every gesture, and even his silence, communicate the overwhelming reality of the Dharma.*

In the sixties it was whispered that enlightened masters sitting in caves in the Himalayas were actually engaged in bringing peace to the world. Such remarks were at the edge of credibility and were usually answered by a "wow." (For a more articulate exposition of this position see Nelson Foster, "The Radical Way," in *Turning Wheel: A Journal of Socially Engaged Buddhism*)

Marcuse ("Love Mystified") criticizes the Govinda paragraph:

> *This does not work, and no new symbolic interpretation can remove the impact of the many centuries of deception and exploitation which has defined the connotation of these words.... this task, if it should help us to find "the way out," is a political task: the silence is not that of the Tibetan or any other monastery, nor of Zen, nor of mystical communion—it is the silence which precedes action, the liberating action, and it is broken by action. The rest is not silence but complacency, or despair, or escape.*

Marcuse accuses Brown of espousing a Totality, a Whole, that "does not exist in any sense or non-sense, and should not even be the vision of the free imagination." Brown sided with the surrealists that the first step to liberation is, indeed, the liberation of the imagination.

> *Poetry, art, imagination, the creator spirit is life itself; the real revolutionary power to change the world; and to change the human body.* (NOB, "Love Mystified: A Reply," in Marcuse, *Negations*)

Brown came to favor the theatrical in political action, that marches should be processions, bearing the pine-cone-topped *thyrsa* of the Dionysian maenads. He called the flamboyant activist/ >>

DP: Why?

NOB: Antinomianism.[6]

>> performer/astrologer Rob Brezsny "my good student." I use Brown's essay "Dionysus in 1990" in my investigation of Burning Man as metapolitical festival:

> Brown recognizes that in the era of HCE ("Here Comes Everybody"), the outcome depends on whether or not the masses settle for vicarious entertainment. Blake's "spectral enjoyment." Spectator. Here, watch the gladiator shed blood, right on your television.
>
> "The Grand Inquisitor is betting that circuses will satisfy. The Dionysian bets the Grand Inquisitor is wrong."

(A/M 197)

Lastly, we might remember that Brown went through a (brief) Maoist phase, when he handed out copies of *The Little Red Book*. For more on Brown as a political revolutionary, see the essay by Christopher Connery in *In Memoriam*, edited by Jerome Neu.

[6] Antinomianism:

> The belief held by various sects, but particularly by radical protestant movements of the 16th and 17th centuries, that certain chosen Christians are by faith or by predestination unable to sin, and are hence set free from the requirement to obey any moral law. Antinomianism is frequently associated with unconventional life styles and sexual practices. (Oxford Dictionary of Philosophy)

Christopher Hill, in *The World Turned Upside Down*, explores antinomianism in such sects as the Diggers and the Ranters in the English Civil War. E. P. Thompson (*Witness Against the Beast: William Blake and the Moral Law*) claims that Blake inherited the antinomian tradition through the Muggletonians. Another outbreak occurred in upstate New York in the 1840s. (Whitney Cross, *The Burned-Over District; The Social and Intellectual History of Enthusiastic Religion in Western New York, 1800-1850*)   <to p.46>

\>\> <from p.45> Antinomianism often accompanies "New Age" movements, at least on their religious fringes (see Martin Green, *Prophets of a New Age, the Politics of Hope from the Eighteenth through the Twenty-First Centuries*, for descriptions of New Age movements in the 1790s, the 1890s, and the 1960s).

Historically, emotional reaction to the antics of the liberated avant-garde have often helped to usher in periods of political repression (the Restoration in England, the National Socialists after the Weimar Republic, and, more recently, the conservative backlash following the 1960s and 1970s in the United States).

Outbursts of flagrant and morally offensive behavior accompany Dionysus with a sort of mythological inevitability. As I have stated elsewhere (and in my *Pharmako* trilogy), it is the *suppression* of Dionysus that leads to real tragedy, the sacrifice of children (as in the "War on Drugs"). Brown, and Euripides, would concur.

7 Wordsworth: left as an exercise for the student. No magic, no epic: perhaps for Milton, the problem is more related to the telescope than to his blank verse. There are three references to Galileo in *Paradise Lost*, the only contemporary figure to so appear.

8 Pagels distinguishes between mere enemies, such as Rome, who may be loved and forgiven, and the heretic, Satan, the apostate *within* the community, for whom no punishment is too severe. She speculates that this distinction may be so deeply wedded with Christianity that it cannot be uprooted. Hence pogroms, and, what I've thought would make a good bumper sticker, "Kill All Fanatics."

9 Alchemically, salamanders are fire.

DP: Gee, I thought that was what was right about 1968. Do you think antinomianism follows Romanticism?

NOB: You can see some of that in Wordsworth. I think there is no epic because there is no magic.[7]

DP: Or because there is no Satan. I read a book by Elaine Pagels, *The Origin of Satan*.

NOB: I don't like Pagels. She has been in my living room, but I saw no signs of Dionysus. Do you have another opinion?

DP: No, but now that the gods are messing with her life, the loss of a child and the loss of her husband, she seems to be taking her subject more seriously and is having a crisis of faith. That I do find interesting. She thinks that the importance of Satan in Christianity may be an irredeemable fault.[8]

NOB: I still see no signs of Dionysus.

(We were crossing a steep grassy hillside. We found a large newt that was crossing the trail and talked a little about salamanders and fire. I mentioned that they hid in the bark of firewood in woodsheds, so that was why you might see them climbing out of a fireplace.[9] Birds were in abundance, and their songs became a backdrop and counterpoint to our conversation.)

DP: Plato said that the soul had wings.

NOB: Yes, that has always bothered me.

DP: Is that the origin of the wings on Christian angels?

NOB: I'm not sure. Angels are hermaphrodites.

DP: I think Christian angels are always male, at least my father thought so. Angels visited Descartes, but he denied them later.

NOB: You have problems with your father.

[10] *Robert Graves: The Laura Riding Years 1926-1940*, by Richard Perceval Graves.

[11] Lou Andreas-Salomé, muse to Nietzsche, Rilke, and Freud. There is a photograph of Lou sitting in a donkey cart holding a whip, and Nietzsche and Paul Rée in front holding the tongue of the cart.

(I told Nobby about the theological arguments that I had with my father in my childhood, how I could never win and would always end up angry. Nobby remarked that "anger is rarely helpful.")

DP: I've been reading a biography of Robert Graves, by his nephew.[10]

NOB: Does it detail his relationship with Laura Riding?

DP: Yes. It was sexual at first, and then Laura moved in with Graves and his wife. When they moved to Majorca, Laura laid down the law that sex was out and that they were moving onto a higher, spiritual plane.

NOB: Yes, I think she dominated him. You should read about Lou Salome.[11]

DP: Maybe Graves' mistake was in missing the hermaphrodite, which led to goddess worship and his masochistic submission, to his domination by Riding.

NOB: How do you see domination?

DP: The stimulants.

NOB: What about the hallucinogens?

DP: Pentecost.

(The trail led through a grove of oaks and buckeyes. I changed the subject and told Nobby that I had been to a Grateful Dead show. Always the voyeur when it came to stories of sex, drugs, and rock and roll, Nobby wanted lots of details.)

DP: If you are really interested in Dionysian Mysteries, you ought to come with me to a show. Joseph Campbell went.

NOB: I wouldn't follow Joseph Campbell anywhere.

DP: We all partook of the sacraments and joined in that special bonding of the collective madness. It healed my back. I haven't had any back pain for three weeks.

12 Nobby's mother, Margarita, was an anthroposophist and a member of an esoteric order (Nobby thought it was the Order of the Golden Dawn). Bookshelf space is very precious to scholars like Brown, the flow of books always exceeding the available space. Even so, almost an entire long shelf in Nobby's office was occupied by the works of Rudolf Steiner. What Nobby did not mention was that he was brought back to Steiner by M. C. Richards, also an anthroposophist.

13 NOB's "father is a blank," but in LB, "Liberty," based on Freud's "all-powerful father," it is the mother who is missing. Where in the anthropological study of "primitive" cultures can one find the "all-powerful father," keeping all the women for himself? If there is any resemblance between early human culture and my own family (at least the distaff side), everyone danced to the tune of the Grandmother.

In an autobiographical essay, Brown states:

> *I remember my mother as being the driving force in the family's involvement in the theosophical counterculture. My father, I believe, had lost the original Presbyterian faith so alive in my memories of Donaghmore. He was not an intellectual. I have called him a straight-forward British patriot. His natural instincts were to conform. But in some incomprehensible way, he went along with my mother, at least in the outward motions.* (In Memoriam: Norman O. Brown, *edited by Jerome Neu.*)

When the father is a blank (and therefore the spectral presence in the text), perhaps the mother is too petrifying to gaze upon.

14 The equation is most explicitly explored in "Fire":

> *A fiery consummation. Not suspense, but end-pleasure; not partial sacrifice (castration), but total holocaust. It is as fire that sex and war and eating and sacrifice are one.* (LB 178)

> *War is war perverted. The problem is not the war but the perversion. And the perversion is a repression; war is sex perverted. "War is energy Enslav'd."* (LB 181)

> *The thing, then, is not to abolish war but to find the true war. Open the hidden Heart in Wars of Mutual Benevolence, Wars of Love.* (LB 182)   >>

NOB: It is the intersection of the exoteric with the esoteric. It is inevitable that I should have to deal with it because of my mother.[12]

(We were ambling across a meadow. I was trying to find a way to pursue the matter of Nobby's mother, but I was too slow.)

NOB: My father is a complete blank. I don't see how he fits into any of what I'm doing.[13]

(I didn't respond.)

NOB: You took your family along to the Grateful Dead?

(Nobby was pretty easy to shock, and I always took pleasure therein. It was my only defense against his own merciless vitriol. Talk of the Grateful Dead led to talk of the sixties.)

NOB: "Make love, not war" won't do. *Love's Body* showed that they were the same thing.[14]

\>> Blake is never far beneath the surface:

Rouze up O Young Men of the New Age! set your foreheads against the ignorant Hirelings! For we have Hirelings in the Camp, the Court, & the University: who would if they could, forever depress Mental & prolong Corporeal War.
(Blake, *Milton*)

Corporeal war is the lowest form of violence, a Satanic parody, the death decreed to those who run away from the true battle.

David Greenham points out that Brown was pursuing unity in contrariety and strife as early as the *Theogony*.

It is Heraclitus who ... [recognizes] that antagonism and reconciliation are intimate and that the difference and unity, notwithstanding the paradox, are one. This one he calls harmony, which is unity in contrariety. But this is not a unity of peace, it is unity in war and strife.... This order is necessarily dynamic, only held together out of strife. What is anathema in Brown's reading of Hesiod is inertia, this is not what is meant by order. Order is a way of allowing creative space; it is a way of permitting difference and unity to belong to each other. This is his definition of Eros. (Greenham, *The Resurrection of the Body*, 32-33)

[15] Brown quotes William James, "Remarks at the Peace Banquet":

> "... [War] is a sacrament. Society would rot without the mystical blood-payment." (James, in *LB* 182)

James was seeking a "moral equivalent" to war, as Brown is seeking the symbolic equivalent. ("You have to negate something to make a statement.") Blake: "War is energy Enslav'd." Brown: Creation is violent:

> Birth is bursting, the shell burst.... War is what happens to the weak, the impotent; so that they might at least be touched with lowest form of violence.... Save us from the literal fire. (*LB* 182)

Brown extends the (neurotic) notion of "self" developed in *Life Against Death* into idolatry:

> Involuted Eros and involuted aggression constitute the "autonomous self" or what passes for individuality in the human species. (*LAD* 129)

> To find the true war, the true sacrament; to avoid idolatry (Mexican sacrifices, Moloch); it is all a question of symbolism. To see the sacrament of war as a false sacrifice is to see the demonic parody, the anti-Christ. To see it is to see through it; to see through it is to burn up the idols. "It is Burnt up the Moment Men cease to behold it." (*LB* 182)

For another perspective, relating war to blood sacrifice, and, ultimately, to human prehistory as prey for carnivores, see Barbara Ehrenreich's *Blood Rites: Origins and History of the Passions of War*.

[16] I wanted to critique the supposed "universality" of war: that the tribal warfare reported by early explorers (such as the Beaver Wars of the 1640s) was the result of pressure waves from colonial incursions, not the normal state of society. The problem is not, as apologists for war like to maintain, "human nature," but "weapons of mass destruction," i.e., the state itself.

[17] Walter F. Otto, *Dionysus: Myth and Cult*:

> Even the animals who accompany him [Dionysus] and in whose forms he himself appears from time to time stand in sharp contrast to one another, with the one group (the bull, the goat, >>

DP: Love is the last socially acceptable form of divine madness.

NOB: Beth goes to bed at nine o'clock, so I watch MTV. All the songs are about love. This automatic bow to love won't do.

DP: But love is a pagan goddess, still being worshipped. Is this not cause for hope?

NOB: No, you have to have war. Without war, there would be nothing left, it would be nihilism.[15]

(I didn't like this.)

DP: I think there is a difference between tribal skirmishing and war.[16]

NOB: "Make love, not war" didn't work. It left out the death instinct.

(I thought Nobby was headed for Dionysus, as in Otto: dismembered bodies littering the hill beside the well of wine and honey.)[17]

NOB: I know from my own life that love and war are the same thing.[18]

>> *the ass) symbolizing fertility and sexual desire, and the other (the lion, the panther, the lynx) representing the most bloodthirsty desire to kill.*

[18] *Make Love not War   III*
Lovers are doves   III.v.
our wars are with our girls
I like her hot   III.viii.
I like her fighting mad
maenad
not peace but a sword
always a battle
feuding fighting and fucking
sadism and masochism:
in love I want to feel pain or to feel her feeling pain
aut tua cum digitis scripta silenda notas.
(Brown, "A Homage to Propertius," in *Caterpillar* #13)

[19] In the introduction to *Simians, Cyborgs, and Women; The Reinvention of Nature,* Haraway writes of *Love's Body:*

> *The only escape from the domination that Brown explored was through fantasy and ecstasy, leaving the body politic unchallenged in its fundamental male supremacy and in its reduction to the dynamic of repression of nature. Brown rejected civilization (the body politic) in order to save the body; the solution necessitated by is root acceptance of Freudian sexual reductionism and the ensuing logic of domination. He turned nature into a fetish worshipped by a total return to it (polymorphous perversity). He betrayed the socialist possibilities of a dialectical theory of the body politic that neither worships nor rejects natural science, that refuses to make nature and its knowledge into a fetish.* (Haraway, 9-10)

Cf., however, even to the Brown of *Life Against Death*:

> *Psychoanalysis, mysticism, poetry, the philosophy of organism, Feuerbach, and Marx—this is a miscellaneous assemblage; but, as Heraclitus said, the unseen harmony is stronger than the seen. Common to all of them is a mode of consciousness that can be called—although the term causes fresh difficulties—the dialectical imagination. By "dialectical" I mean an activity of consciousness struggling to circumvent the limitations imposed by the formal-logical law of contradiction.* (*LAD* 318-319)

[20] *Be Here Now*, by Ram Dass (Richard Alpert), 1971: as close to being a "Hippie Bible" as there ever was. Alpert was converted when he gave Neem Karoli Baba three tablets of LSD, who swallowed them and was seemingly impervious to their effects. Alpert evidently thought this proved that Baba was "enlightened." According to Clark Heinrich (*Strange Fruit,* 21), however, the guru Neem Baba simply palmed the pills.

(I was too off balance to interrogate, which was probably part of Nobby's intent. I tried to warn about sophistry; that I wanted to distinguish mere violence from corporate war, state sponsored criminality, but Nobby didn't budge.)

DP: Okay, Love is ideology. I'll give you that.

NOB: Donna Haraway is of your generation, she was in a complex relationship. When Donna Haraway talks about love, I listen.[19]

DP: (Ready to attack) NOB and Marcuse based their whole programs on the thesis that Eros freed could subdue Thanatos. But we know that libertines can be brutal criminals.

NOB: That doesn't disprove it. It can be refuted with high philosophy.

(More walking. I was wondering what is meant by "high philosophy.")

NOB: There was no myth: that was the problem with 1968. The sixties were not religious.

DP: I don't agree with you. Look at the pages of the *San Francisco Oracle*. It was called spirituality, not religion. It was naive, but very enthusiastic, if you know what I mean.

NOB: Enthusiasm must be understood as religious. But do you mean *Be Here Now*, which I have, the Indian thing?[20]

DP: That was part of it. But it was both East Indian and American Indian. And then there were the Pranksters. At the Be-In, the Gathering of the Tribes, on the platform were Allen Ginsberg, Gary Snyder, Timothy Leary, Alan Watts, and Michael McClure. Kesey should have been there but I think he was on the lam in Mexico.

NOB: What was WRONG with the sixties? What was missing?

[21] I told Nobby about an encounter that I had had with Manson's Thirteenth Family in 1967, involving a mythical Lear jet filled with four hundred mythical kilos of marijuana. I watched five hippie dealers cut twenty thousand dollars worth of hundred dollar bills in half so that both sides of the transaction would be sure to meet at the specified location. Needless to say, neither the kilos nor the other half of the cut bills ever appeared.

[22] Hysteria → hypnotism (eyes) → mass psychology → fascism.

> *The actor is exhibitionist. To shew is to show the genital; to fascinate; to make the spectator a woman. Even as the hard look or phallic eye of the hypnotist (a Cyclopean erection) transfixes his subject.* (LB 124)

Fascism < L. *fasces*: the bundle of rods and axe carried to the highest magistrate to scourge and behead a criminal, but also sorcery and witchcraft. L. *fascinum* is a binding spell cast by the eyes or tongue, but also the phallus, the *membrum virile*, worn as an amulet as protection against the *mal occhio*, the evil eye. Phallic herms were used as doorknockers for the same reason, as simple *cornu* are worn today. (Testicles are only the *witness*.)

> *The naked truth. Woe is me, for I am undone: for mine eyes have seen the Queen. All knowledge is guilty knowledge, and the consequence is flight; a divided self, alien horns or alienation; a double nature, or schizophrenia; the timid heart of a stag.* ("Actaeon," A/M, 41)

Lawrence Di Stasi, in *Mal Occhio: The Underside of Vision* (140-141), takes a Jungian approach but also quotes Brown:

> *...the project of every modern human is to make the unconscious conscious, is to reunite as far as possible with all the unconscious contents which humans have been denying these last three thousand years. This would amount to the recall of all those projections both evil and good—projections analogous to the one which animates mal occhio by envisioning evil eyes and envy "out there" when in fact they reside mainly within—which have threatened to make the twentieth century, with its scapegoats in the concentration camps and gulags, the century of mass projection and thereby mass murder.... And in those terms, as elucidated by Norman O. Brown, one might predict a union that would move toward* >>

DP: We underestimated the forces of reaction.

NOB: It was not a Millennium and it was not a New Age.

DP: It was Dionysus.

NOB: It was Dionysus and it came and went.

DP: There was some naivety that way, that Dionysus is always love and light. We didn't understand, for a while, that the same power could drive people to become slaves of mind-controllers.

NOB: Or to kill.[21]

(More walking, through a copse of oaks. The thread moved to Nietzsche, then to Christ and to Nobby's latest paper, "Love Hath Reason," which he said was "too Christian." I agreed with him, somewhat. Nobby thought the address was too somber, and recited a long quote from Euripides, in Greek. But he wanted to get back on track.)

NOB: If I went to a show, would I have to ingest drugs?

DP: Well, you wouldn't HAVE to. There would be so many other people doing it that you would probably get a contact high. I don't think there is any scientific explanation for the contact high, but it certainly does occur.

NOB: I would look in Freud's writing on hysteria. Fascination/Fascism. It has to do with the eyes: Oedipus the King was blinded, and that means testicles. You might take note.[22]

>> *ending what has been called the "tyranny of genital organization." By this is meant that exclusive concentration of libido or energy in the genital, a concentration made compulsive by anxiety and fear of death, which is ultimately the fear of separation from the protecting mother; and which by a paradoxical reaction leads to the fantastic project to become "independent of the totality conceived of as the mother principle."*

See also my discussion of the evil eye (in relation to harmel, *Peganum harmala*) in *Pharmako/Gnosis*, 179-203.

[23] *Derkomai*: to look, to see.

> *Our thesis will be that the evil eye is the ghostly eye of the slain dragon—the dragon's revenge, or curse.... The evil eye is the dry spring, or the well that fails. The spring is life, inspiration, and prophecy: thus the mantis is the python, who is Typhoon, the dragon.... The dragon's water is soma, nectar, milk—true treasure. But when the dragon is killed we are left with the withering— she whose glance is awful.* (Pendell, *Pharmako/Gnosis*, 184)

[24] Cf.

> *Identification with the representative person, whom we "look up to," takes place through the eye.... The primal scene is the original theater; parental coitus is the archetypal show; the original distance is between child and parent.* (*LB* 122)

[25] Thus enters Dionysus:

> *Something more elemental*
> *the hour of the beast—*"pawses"   [*FW* 221]
> It darkles, (tinct, tint) all this our funnaminal world
> *Not Pater noster but* **Panther monster.**   [*FW* 244]
> *Pan-ther: all beast.*
> *When the leopards break into the temple and drink the wine from the sacred chalice.*
> *The hour of the beast, or the barbarian*
> (*CT* 61)

[26] *FW* 160.

[27] *FW* 353.

[28] *"Actaeon, the sacred heart, hart."* (*A/M* 31)

There are really four puns in "Actaeon": *mors*, as mortal, mortuary, mortification, morsel, mordant, remorse; serf = cerf; hart = heart; and various plays on horn.

DP: (Keeps quiet, not sure where this is going.)

NOB: The best is "Mass Psychology," not *Totem and Taboo* or *Moses and Monotheism*. "Mass Psychology" also contains that silly story of the brothers, but it has madness—the hysteria in the girl's school. It's Dionysian. In *Totem and Taboo*, and *Moses and Monotheism*, the contestants are all rational: they behave reasonably, even if lacking in vision. It's Apollonian.

(I was in front at this point and led us in under some trees.)

NOB: How do you see the difference between Christ and Dionysus?

DP: Sheep and goats. Goat's eyes are slit, like snake eyes.

NOB: Eyes are draco, eye magic, *derkomai*.[23]

DP: Some say the universe was created by a one-eyed dragon trying to see itself.[24]

NOB: I think the universe began in chaos.

DP: So we have two theories of Genesis: Chaos and Narcissism.

NOB: I think Joyce is important. Farce. The Christians thought they were in a tragedy, but it was really a farce.[25]

> The poignt of fun where I am crying to arrive you at.[26]

DP: *"Līlā,"* playfulness, is important here, but can you laugh at death? Is not death in a privileged position?

NOB: *The abnihilisation of the etym.*[27]

DP: You based "Actaeon" on a pun.[28]

[29] Phylogeny is a formal system, grammatical, like geometry. Language is a "wild" system, temporal rather than eternal, where Freud, Joyce, and augury come together:

> In puns, "two words get on top of each other and become sexual"; in metaphor, two become one. What God hath joined no philosophy can put asunder. ("Freedom," LB, 252)

And, Brown again:

> Dei dialectus soloecismus—*the dialect of God is solecism.*
> *God does not speak good English.*
> *Not Atticism but solecism.*
> *Barbarism.*
> (CT 63)

On a later walk I told Nobby how a friend had criticized me for placing "Pan" in apposition to "everything." Nobby told me that I was in good company, that Milton and Plato had done the same thing. Greenham, in *The Resurrection of the Body*, quotes the relevant passage from *Cratylus* on his first page: Pan, the son of Hermes, as the one who expresses *all* things, is speech—half goat (*tragikon*) and half smooth, half rough and false and living among the masses and half divine and true and living among the gods. Greenham points out that Brown begins his work at the meeting of the rough and the smooth. The junction is of course the *pharmakon*, the poison and the remedy.

[30] Augury means the world is a book, a book of ciphers, signatures.

> *The speech of birds*
> *shamans*
> *a little bird tells them*
> (NOB, "Inauguration")

[31] The fine point is the difference between "meaningless chance" and poetry: the active creation of meaning.

NOB: I made it a rule not to distinguish between true and false etymology. Lib: liberation, libido. Freya.[29]

DP: *Freude*.

NOB: Good. And Freud, of course. *Freude* to Freud is not true etymology. False etymology is chance.

DP: Tea leaves.[30]

NOB: If you accept tea leaves you let in everything. No preordination: that's chance.[31]

DP: It comes down to bastardy versus eugenics.

NOB: You can't say bastard now. This is not Shakespeare's time. Bastardy was one of his hang-ups. Besides, fatherhood is an illusion.

DP: What about DNA?

NOB: You mean they can tell for sure?

DP: Yes. (Or so they say.)

NOB: I'll have to think about that ... I've been involved with this question of legitimate/illegitimate from the beginning, for forty years, and what good has it done?

(We walked a few more steps and Nobby answered his own question.)

NOB: It led me to Joyce, and also Vico.

DP: So you are setting Freud against Joyce and Vico. It's a short jump to Gurdjieff.

NOB: But we don't really need him, why do you bring him up?

DP: *All and Everything, Beelzebub's Tales to His Grandson*. His reveling is into the occult. I do that also. How is that so different from Vico?

NOB: Vico is in the canon. Gurdjieff is *not* in the canon.

³² And NOB criticized Cage's "Writing Through Finnegans Wake":

Writing for the Fifth Time through Finnegans Wake
getting rid of the syntax
getting rid of the cadence
getting rid of the puns
(NOB, "John Cage," *Aufgabe* #5, 86)

To ensure indeterminacy with respect to its performance, a composition must be determinate of itself. If this indeterminacy is to have a non-dualistic nature, each element of the notation must have a single interpretation rather than a plurality of interpretations. (John Cage, *Silence*, 38, quoted in NOB, "John Cage," *Aufgabe* #5)

³³ συνταξις: the formations of soldiers, the order of battle.

³⁴ *At any rate intellectuals should watch their language*
The critical judgement
        Which separates the sheep from the goats
            We and They
Critical judgement is party or sect formation
        Is schism of the one body
And projection of part of ourselves
(FPTM, 212-213)

(More walking. I didn't like this business of "the canon." Nobby mentioned that, after many years, he was reading Finnegans Wake *again, by this point a redundant pronouncement.)*

> NOB: Joyce only had to face the novel, unlike Freud. He did have an easier problem. What is the root of "revel"?

(It's "rebel," but we couldn't get to it on the trail, though we did reject "reveal." We walked for a bit, then Nobby returned to the thread.)

> NOB: Cage criticized Joyce for not breaking free from syntax.[32]

> DP: I don't think that's fair. There can be non-syntactical language: poetry. Is rebelling against syntax, against "grow up and get in line, man," merely juvenile individualism?

> NOB: Syntax is the army, the formations of soldiers.[33]

> DP: So what's the problem with syntax?

> NOB: Soul. Ego is implicit in language and we have to get rid of that.

> DP: (Things were moving fast) That's a *very* sixties sentiment.

> NOB: Maybe Dionysus can transcend the difference.

(More walking. I was trying to digest it all. Nobby returned to sheep and goats.)

> NOB: I don't like sheep and goats, that's Judgment. Would you, aside from the metaphor, divide humanity into sheep and goats?[34]

> DP: (Thinks) No.

> NOB: Jesus said judge not, but at other places I think he makes a distinction between sheep and goats, and prefers the sheep.

[35] A rather uncharacteristic lapse into what Brown elsewhere calls "necromancy":

> The quest for the historical Jesus: it is either literally true, including literal miracles, or not true at all. The historical Jesus, a unique event in unilinear time, what has that to do with us here now? The very argument which establishes his miraculous divinity separates our humanity from his divinity. (LB 213)

[36] Robert Graves and Joshua Podro, tried to reconstruct the "authentic" gospel of the Jerusalem Church (*The Nazarene Gospel*). Stephen Mitchell (*The Gospel of Jesus*) also collected what he thought were the "true" sayings of Jesus. Thomas Jefferson did the same thing. Elaine Pagels summarized the historical events surrounding each of the Gospels in *The Origin of Satan*.

[37] Marcuse stated this quite sharply:

> Brown takes great pains to state again and again that the religious symbolism is to be interpreted symbolically, in the other direction, as it were. Sexual potency is restored at Pentecost; speech resexualized (p.251); knowledge made carnal, copulation of subject and object (p.249); and the spirit is phallic (p.224) — merger of Christ and Dionysus. But the one stays with the other, and the new emphasis does not suffice to reverse the established direction: sexualization of the spirit is also spiritualization of sexuality, and sexuality itself becomes symbolic.... Brown's consistent attempt to convey, against overwhelming odds, the new nonrepressive interpretation of the old repressive symbols cannot undo the association of the spirit with the Spirit, the resurrection of the body with the Resurrection. (Herbert Marcuse, "Love Mystified")

DP: Yes, it's in the Scripture.

NOB: I think Jesus missed there. He was too influenced by Jewish apocalyptic thought and eschatology.

DP: But radical Judaism, not mainstream. The Last Judgment was a big deal for the Essenes, not so much for the Pharisees or the Sadducees. Maybe the problem with Christianity is John the Baptist.

NOB: How?

DP: Baptism.

NOB: That the baptized were sheep and the unbaptized goats?

DP: Yes.

NOB: I don't think I have a problem with John the Baptist. (Pause, more walking.) I would like to consider what Jesus really said, apart from the ecclesiasticism.[35]

DP: Graves tried to do that. And Stephen Mitchell.[36]

(We were in an open area and looking down on the canyon of the San Lorenzo River.)

DP: It seems that you want to contend with the Christians on their own turf, by their own rules.

NOB: There is ample evidence that that cannot be done.[37]

DP: Maybe you are right about using Joyce.

NOB: Even Joyce is too Christian: too much Vico.

DP: Do you think that there may be a problem with trying to redefine symbols?

NOB: What do you mean?

DP: That in trying to redefine the symbols of the dominant religion, it will only end up enhancing the hegemony. That the orthodox, being in the majority, will co-opt the attempts to redefine the symbols, and that it will

[38] Cf.

> *The reality principle is about over*
> *Thought as work can be buried in machines and computers*
> *The work left to be done is to bury thought; quite a job*
> *To put thought underground*
> *   As communication network, sewage system, power lines*
> *So that wildness can come above ground*
> *Technological rationality can be put to sleep*
> *So that something else can awaken in the human mind*
> *Something like the god Dionysus*
> *Something which cannot be programmed*
> (FPTM, 208)

[39] I was referring to what might best be called "ousiaphanic" plants and drugs, not narcotics.

> *But the Greeks, who gave us Apollo, also gave us the alternative, Nietzsche's Dionysus. Dionysus is not dream but drunkenness; not life kept at a distance and seen through a veil but life complete and immediate.* (LAD 174-175)

Compare with Brown in an interview with Warren Bennis:

> Bennis: *Would you say that the widespread use of LSD and other hallucinogenic drugs has given the present generation an unprecedented acquaintance with the Dionysian style of life? Some have claimed that LSD creates instant polymorphous perversity.*
>
> Brown: *I don't accept the standard use of the word "hallucinogenic." I don't like hallucinogenic things such as the mass media with their advertising and political campaigns, with their managed and manufactured news. I don't use drugs. However, it is obvious that we need a breakthrough to a visionary reality, poetic vision. Surely the Second Coming is at hand, when your young men shall see visions.*
>
> (Sam Keen, *Voices and Visions*, 1974)

just give orthodoxy more strength by helping to perpetuate the symbols. Sometimes I wonder if some symbols may be unredeemable, and the best thing to do is just hope they will fade away.

NOB: Christianity will disappear when America disappears.

DP: Ah, then there is hope.

NOB: Milton tried to get beyond Christianity and failed. Blake tried and failed.

DP: Nietzsche succeeded.

NOB: But "Christ versus Dionysus" is not the last word.

DP: Maybe Dionysus/Christ is wild/domestic?[38]

NOB: Be careful about "wild," don't elevate it. That just gets to Wordsworth.

DP: I disagree. Wild is also inebriation, which is drugs.

NOB: (Derisively) We always get back to that.[39]

(We had left the trail at this point, and were trying to make our way cross country. We walked in silence for awhile through some oaks and then emerged back onto open meadow. When I stopped to admire the scenery of a canyon that opened below us, Nobby passed me and started talking about his family life. We talked about our children and fatherly concerns about our daughters. Nobby was much more forthcoming than was usual for him. The talk turned to marriage.)

NOB: Marriage ... I'm not sure what to say about marriage.

DP: Love and/or Marriage, start with that. Astrology, you know, puts love and marriage in different houses.

NOB: Yes. Marriage is about children.

DP: Yes, and property.

[40] Dante, assigned as homework.

[41] Laurel (Petrarch's Laura) as "pure" spiritual love. Myrtle (Venus) as carnal love.

> Love's best retreat. *The spiritualization of sensuality is love: a great triumph over Christianity, says Nietzsche. Sensuality is not abolished, but fulfilled.*
> No white nor red was ever seen
> So amorous as this lovely green. ("Daphne," A/M, 19)

[42] Denis de Rougemont: *Love in the Western World,* on courtly love, the Cathars, the tension between marriage and romantic love that is outside the marriage, and the perversion of individual passion into the collective passion of war:

> *From desire to death via* passion—*such has been the road taken by European romanticism ... inasmuch as our notion of love enfolds our notion of woman, it is linked with a theory of the* fruitfulness of suffering *which encourages or obscurely justifies in the recesses of the Western mind a liking for war.*

Geoffrey Gorer ("Falling in Love," in *Eros, Agape, and Philia,* edited by Alan Soble) states that the capacity to fall passionately in love seems to develop spontaneously in a few individuals in all human societies that have been described.

[43] M. C. Richards, the poet and potter. Brown met Richards at a poetry reading at Wesleyan, April 19, 1960. The poet was probably Charles Olson, because both Olson and Richards were at the get-together after the reading, talking in the Brown's kitchen. Richards knew Olson from Black Mountain College. She had read *Life Against Death* on advice from John Cage, another mutual friend.

Richards called Brown several days later and they began a correspondence. The tone of the letters warmed quickly, and emotional intimacies were exchanged along with matters intellectual. It seems to have been mostly, if not entirely, a literary affair. During the months that followed they spent at least one afternoon together, walking in the woods, but mostly the meetings they planned were later canceled by Brown. The final break came in January of 1961, Brown writing that he needed distance, and even adding *"noli me tangere."* >>

NOB: There is a problem with the family. I saw it in *Life Against Death*.

DP: Marriage has gotten too much love mixed up in it. That creates a tension.

NOB: For love, you have to read *La Vita Nuova*.[40]

DP: Or Petrarch: "Who really desires laurel, or myrtle either?"[41]

(We talked about the tension between love and marriage. Some reference was made to de Rougemont.[42] We kept walking but at a slower pace and side by side.)

NOB: I was once in love with M. C. Richards. She was an anthroposophist.[43]

>> My own feeling is that Richards was very important to Brown. Brown was searching for "love's body," and something beyond the world of the academy, and Richards was the fleshly embodiment of the whole alternative "scene" of poetry, music, and the arts. She gave him reading lists and introduced him to a number of sources and topics that remained important to him the rest of his life, including Buddhism, surrealism, Owen Barfield, and other authors who later appear in *Love's Body*. She was, I think, Nobby's Laura, and "Daphne" surely resonates with her presence. Richards also had Brown reading Steiner, which may have been what finally gave him cold feet (M. C. even wrote to Nobby's mother, Margarita, hoping to find an ally who could explain Brown's "distance").

Most importantly, Brown was uneasy with his new notoriety as a "radical." M. C. challenged this radicalism—she was the real thing, a living part of the alternative lifestyle, and comfortable therein. With M. C. securing the left flank, Brown was able to return to the center, where he could be the Old Testament prophet, preaching hellfire to the idol worshippers and pointing to the Promised Land.

[44] On the other hand, Dionysus married Ariadne, who had been abandoned by Theseus. And married women formed the core of the Dionysian revelers.

[45] For which he has been criticized by many on the "left" as being passé. Even Beth Brown, who did so much to maintain the regularity that Nobby depended upon, was criticized for her conventionality. Gayatri Spivak, commenting on talking to Nobby at his home while Beth served them tea, quipped to a class on Derrida in the History of Consciousness program, "So what do I deconstruct, what he is saying or that Beth is serving tea?" (Followed by the snickers of those, I suppose, too liberated for such graciousness.)

[46] I've thought about this many times over the years, and whether or not renunciation is cowardice. One year I wrote this:

That cup—you took one draught,
left the rest
> *for a lifetime's paean*
to love
> *at the fringe.*
Did you sense
> *with inner hunch*
you couldn't have
> *both, or*
did the stakes seem
> *too seductive, too*
full of risk—
> *to follow*
that goat god
> *off the trail*
to the bad boy's home
> *in a woman's curl.*

(Nobby looked to see if I recognized the name.)

DP: Oh yes, *Centering*.

NOB: I met her when I was at Wesleyan ...

(I was ready to hear more, but just assumed that it would come out in time. I tried to maintain the thread.)

DP: Marriage doesn't seem very ... Dionysian.[44]

NOB: It was a seventeenth century problem: how to love the soul and not deny the body. And this is the problem that has run out now. Or, their solution is now exhausted.

(Nobby had gradually come to know the principal actors in my own complex domestic drama, especially the women, and had met several of them—one who had joined us for a three-way walk, and another when he and Beth had come for dinner. I filled him in on some of the romantic details. Some of the arrangements he found hilariously funny; others seemed to bewilder him and I had to repeat certain stories over and over.)

DP: Okay. Your turn.

NOB: My life was very conventional.[45]

DP: (Silent walking. I didn't probe, just waited.)

NOB: Having a conventional marriage enabled me to be free intellectually. I don't think that I could have gone all the places I did otherwise.[46]

(Another minute or two of walking. A jay was squawking. Nobby brought the talk back to the Grateful Dead.)

NOB: You took your daughter?! You dared do that? I would never.

DP: They provide a safe space to surrender to agape. We sixties hippies were serious about our madness. We didn't just taste around the edges, we embraced it.

[47] Nygren: *Eros and Agape*. Describing the Gnostic love-feast:

> *In the oldest Greek poetry Eros appears as the driving force in the Cosmic process; and it is just this original function of Eros that Agape assumes in Gnosticism.*
>
> *From these fundamental principles ethical consequences can be drawn in two opposite directions, ascetic and antinomian, and examples of both are found in Gnosticism....*
>
> *This is the darkest point in the whole history of the Christian idea of love. In Gnosticism, Christian Agape is drawn into the syncretistic whirlpool of late antiquity, is dragged down and associated with the lowest and most repulsive cult forms in the history of religion. It is not merely transformed into Eros, not merely into vulgar Eros, but into the very lowest forms of this.* (Nygren, *Eros and Agape*, Part II)

(Epiphanius' descriptions of a group sex scene follow.)

[48] "Millennium" as a crisis cult, as in Weston La Barre, *the Ghost Dance*. La Barre's premise is that all religions are crisis cults, beginning with the infantile personality of the shaman. See my "Iboga" chapter in *Pharmako/Gnosis*, 294-305.

[49] Much more than merely survive. Who does not believe in an unconscious? Who doesn't believe in repression? "Educated" professors will say "No one takes Freud seriously today" while completely accepting his essential cosmology. Actually, there are a lot of people who don't believe in the unconscious, in repression, or in the significance of childhood traumas, real or imaginary: loosely, they are called "animists." *We've Had a Hundred Years of Psychotherapy and the World's Getting Worse,* by James Hillman and Michael Ventura, explores some of these ideas. Jung tried to reach the spirits with his "collective unconscious."

(NOB just nodded, and said something about agape, and Nygren. I hadn't read Nygren.[47])

DP: Freud's approach won't do, it's just looking from the outside.

NOB: And you are looking from the inside, that's why neither of us are going to succeed.

(We were climbing at this point and the exertion eclipsed our conversation for a while.)

NOB: I have to get over negativity, being negative.

DP: (Wryly) Why? Is this some problem with your mother?

NOB: (Giving me a quick glance) I do have a problem with my mother, but how did you get to that from being negative?

DP: Minus sign, vulva, just a divination. — *interpretation!*

NOB: You have to negate something to make a statement.

DP: Okay, apocalypse equals millennium.[48]

NOB: No. Use etymology. And I say that for a reason: Joyce. That Joyce's method might work, where philosophy à la Pagels would not.

DP: A flower bursting open, a power busting pen.

NOB: Good. What have you been reading?

DP: Biology, mathematics.

NOB: Good!

DP: And I'm trying to get the lay of the land around Freud, an overview, so I can fit things in.

NOB: I'm worried about your academic tendencies.

DP: I've also been reading Crews on Freud. His attacks are pretty devastating.

NOB: Freud will survive, trust me.[49]

50 The basic premise of *Life Against Death* is that all human culture is neurosis, therefore the proper application of psychoanalysis is to history and culture.

Still, just as *research*, I think NOB should have tried analysis. But maybe he wanted to prove that he was Freud's equal, able to analyze himself.

51 For instance, both the Freudian unconscious and the spirit world are "timeless."

52 As if "science" knew anything more about death than did Socrates! There is a Zen koan that addresses death rather directly:

Doushuai asked:

"When you have freed yourself from birth and death, you will know where to go. After your body has separated into the four elements—earth, water, fire, wind—where do you go?"

DP: It's not clear that it has much therapeutic efficacy.

NOB: Oh, I don't support psychotherapy at all.[50]

DP: On what I'm calling the "poison path," it's not childhood traumas, but what the gods are angry about. My point is that the two systems are mappable, that psychoanalysis could be mapped as a subset of animistic shamanism; that pre-literate cultures have very sophisticated methods of psychological healing.[51]

NOB: I think they are all afraid of death.

DP: (Infuriated by the dismissal) But what about the warriors? You can't say they are afraid of death?

(Nobby walked on with his chin in the air, quite pleased with the effect he had created and implying that my attempts at rebuttal were beneath notice.)

DP: Okay, but I would say that they are afraid of the dead; that's not the same as being afraid of death.

(Nobby let this stand. But I was still annoyed by his assumption of superiority.)

DP: Science may say that there is nothing after death, but that is just where science becomes superstition.[52]

(The shadows had lengthened. We had turned and were evidently heading back toward the car.)

NOB: How is your writing going?

DP: Not well.

NOB: I'm not surprised.

DP: What do you mean?

NOB: You're very repressed.

DP: (Annoyed) You think that I am repressed?

NOB: (Laughing heartily) Your aggressive impulses are so repressed they are twisted into a circle.

⁵³ *The necessity of farce or* Finnegans Wake *in order to have our archetypes without Jungian solemnity or Yeatsian occultism.* (CT 55)

⁵⁴ In *LAD* Brown criticized Jung for retreating from the body and from repression.

⁵⁵ Beauty is truth, truth beauty.

⁵⁶ Blake, *Jerusalem. Love's Body* is arranged four by four—I'm sure Nobby was thinking of Blake's fourfold vision. In "Daphne" and "Actaeon" Brown followed Dante and the structure of *Ovide Moralisé*, that each story should have four levels of meaning: the literal, that tells you what happened; the allegorical, that gives you doctrine, what to believe; the moral, that tells you what to do; and the anagogic, that tells you where you are going. Single Vision is idolatry.

⁵⁷ Any system has to deal with that question sooner or later ...

⁵⁸ (Yeah, right.)

Poet Duncan McNaughton, comparing Brown to Robert Duncan, once said to me: "Brown makes a mistake that Duncan would never make, that no poet would make."

As well as McNaughton and I were able to reconstruct the conversation, McNaughton was referring to the reification of metaphor. Herbert Marcuse, in as close as he comes to poetic criticism in "Love Mystified," made a similar point when he stated:

> But the imagery is not enough; it must become saturated with its reality: symbolism must recapture that which it symbolizes. The king must be shown not only as father but as king, that is to say, as master and lord; war and competition and communication must be shown not only as copulation but as war and business and speech. Unless the analysis takes the road of return from the symbolic to the literal, from the illusion, it remains ideological, replacing one mystification by another.... Poetry is made in history, and makes history.

Actually, Brown's "mistake" is not a mistake: it's just that Brown is a *metaphysical* poet. (Of course, when it comes to taking metaphor as *reality*, the wager is a little bigger.)

(I had given Nobby my table of contents, and a copy of the psychoactive plant mandala I had constructed.)

>NOB: Your organization is on the level of archetypes. I'm worried about your Jungian tendencies.[53]
>
>DP: What is the problem with Jung?
>
>NOB: Something vague that explains a lot, something transcendental that you can't really define.[54]
>
>DP: If it's mythology, that part would be okay, what bothers me is their imperialism—they explain everyone else's myths in terms of their own system, but then posit their own cosmology as "scientific," and therefore "real."
>
>NOB: Jung's system would really be better than Freud for what I do, but I don't like his style.[55]
>
>DP: You have a point. The best parts of so many Jungian books are the chapter titles and the illustrations.
>
>NOB: Your mandala is Jungian.
>
>DP: You think it should be Freudian?
>
>NOB: No. Freud is a determinist, that won't do. Marxist determinism won't do. John Cage, chance, says "eschew all systems."
>
>DP: "I must Create a System, or be enslav'd by another Mans."[56]

(Nobby wasn't about to contest that one. I felt emboldened.)

>DP: Do you believe in an external reality?[57]
>
>NOB: (Thinks) No.
>
>DP: But how many are really interested in metaphysics? Are you interested in metaphysics?
>
>NOB: No, not much.[58]

January 1994

59 I told Nobby of the method I had learned from Gary Snyder. Gary cut up paper that was used on one side into 3x5 cards with his paper cutter. The idea was that the cards were wholly free—they were available in unlimited quantity and they didn't cost anything, therefore they could be used to write down any passing thought or idea, no matter how trivial it seemed, without being wasteful.

60 That is, there are so many—one can't read them all. Even for a specialized subject. Great intellectuals like Nobby seemed to have a canny knack for finding the gold, for separating the wheat from the chaff. I'm not sure this knack can be taught, though this is the ideal goal of education. Mostly, the results of such attempts merely result in a "canon." Nobby used the "canon," as far as that goes, but I was asking something else. Maybe "how do you know which books *not* to read" would have been more to the point.

61 Huzza!

(That was fair. I felt more or less the same. We were nearing where we had parked the car. I wanted some practical stuff.)

DP: How did you do the writing of *Love's Body*?

NOB: I used 5x8 cards. I'd collect the quotes on the cards by subject, then I laid them all out on the floor.[59]

DP: How do you decide which books to read?[60]

NOB: Well, I use the classics: Shakespeare.

DP: That is duly noted. I was really referring to newer material.

NOB: I look for the fire in a book.

(We had reached the car and were driving back toward Pasatiempo. The discussion veered to Heraclitus. From Heraclitus, we got to music, and from music to "poison." Poison brought us to my common ground with the works of NOB, which is where we were when we got back to Nobby's driveway.)

DP: It's so difficult to get it right.

NOB: It was more important that I melt the *arcanum* than to be right.[61]

(Nobby got out of the car.)

NOB: Good walk. See you again.

WILDER RANCH, JULY 1995

(I hadn't seen Nobby since before the release of Pharmako/Poeia, about a month. As I usually did, I glanced at the books on the table by the door; this is where he put the books that he was returning to the library. One was M. H. Abrams, Natural Supernaturalism. *I picked it up.)*

NOB: It's wrong. Abrams doesn't understand Dionysus.

DP: You know, you have a rather easy way of judging everything. Too easy. If it's Dionysus, it's good, if it's not, it's wrong. You judge everything by how it fits into your system. Gary [Snyder] has that ability—being able to fit everything he reads into his system—but your perversity is much worse.

NOB: I'm older than Gary is. At my age it is necessary to have an obsession to be able to continue at all.

(I put the book back on the table.)

NOB: Now if we look at you and drugs ...

(So the personal attacks had begun before we were even out the door. Nobby was building up to a summary dismissal of DP—but when he saw that I anticipated it and was already laughing, he had to admit laughter himself and didn't bother to continue. The sparring was complete, the foils had been drawn and tested, and we were both pleased with the result: we were en garde and ready to begin.)

NOB: Let's take your car.

DP: (We always took my car) Okay.

(It was a beautiful day, cool and gusty with scattered clouds, so we decided to go to Wilder Ranch, up Empire Grade above and to the west of the University property. A lot of the Wilder Ranch hike was over exposed meadows that sloped to the southwest, so we wouldn't usually hike there if the day was hot and sunny, preferring, instead, one of the shady hikes such as Fall Creek. But today was perfect.

We were driving toward the university, on the west side of Santa Cruz. I had left a little booklet that I had found at a used bookstore in the side pocket of the passenger door in the hopes that Nobby might find it. He did. It was How to Bluff Your Way in Philosophy.*)*

NOB: Ah ha! I've discovered your secret.

DP: You've caught me. Art is doing much with little.

NOB: Yes. I've been reading Emily Dickinson.

DP: Say more.

NOB: I'm also reading Camille Paglia's essay in *Sexual Personae,* and Susan Howe, *My Emily Dickinson.* I'm afraid that Susan Howe has been overly influenced by Brown. She's writing using some of the techniques of *Love's Body.* I'm uncomfortable being a model. But *you* might like her book.

DP: Yes, I might. I saw that you added one of her poems at the end of "Daphne." Good addition. Do you like Paglia?

NOB: Yes, I sent her a fan letter for *Sexual Personae*. She's the only one of your generation who is saying something. So they all dump on her.

DP: I knew her friend Bruce Benderson. We drove across the country together from Berkeley to New York for the big peace march in 1965, along with Larry Beinhart and another man we called John the Crutch. We were all in a big green panel truck. We dropped him off at Harpur College ... At least I think he made the trip with us. That was the sixties and some parts are a little hazy. There's a funny story I could tell about Bruce ... Oh yes, (laughing), on that trip I met my first Marxist-Freudian. I had forgotten that. She was John the Crutch's aunt.

(Nobby liked my stories, and he especially wanted to know about the mysterious aunt, but I didn't have a lot to tell him.)

DP: I was only eighteen and just at the beginning of my education. I don't think I had ever met either a Marxist OR a Freudian. These were both terms of great mystery. I didn't know what either of them meant, but they sounded like something very esoteric and very far out, and I thought that therefore she would understand me.

NOB: What was she like?

DP: I was sort of disappointed. She lived in the Village, but it was a very ordinary looking apartment and she seemed kind of sad and pained. Pathos. And she spent most of her time talking to her nephew, not to me.

NOB: (Smiling) So you found NOB. This is *so* Oedipal.

(We had reached our destination and I parked the car along the side of the road. I had another book in my pack that I wanted to show him: Michel Serres, The Parasite. *I had been looking for the book in every used book store I could find for over a year. It was a beautiful, clean first edition and I could tell that Nobby was envious.)*

[1] The question relates to what I call the "poison path" in *Pharmako/Poeia*. The poison path is the "Way of Eve," accepting forbidden knowledge, wagering that *expecting* the citizenry (an armed citizenry) to be morally responsible encourages such, while paternalistic control, treating the citizenry as children, stunts social maturation. Are there limits? What about the new law that prohibits the sale or possession of books about bomb-making? Similar laws are being introduced in regard to drug information on the Internet.

[2] Following Vico and Euripides:

> This is the Dionysian turn to the common man.
> τὸ πλῆθος ὅ τι τὸ φαυλότερον
> ἐνόμισε χρῆταίτε, τόδ'ἂν δεχοίμαν.
> The customs and beliefs of the vulgar are normative.
> The mass line. (CT 108)

Or, Dodds' translation: "Whatever the simple many have taken as their rule and usage, that I would accept." (Dodds, *Bacchae*, 430)

> The conflict between low-brow mass culture and the high-brow avant-garde will not go away. Even Whitman, in Democratic Vistas, sees himself as facing "the appalling dangers of universal suffrage in the United States." ("Revisioning Historical Identities," *A/M*, 160)

Dionysus/Demos stands contra Plato of the *Republic*, and contra Hobbes. In "The Turn to Spinoza," Brown connects Spinoza's fields of interacting forces with Freud's (Dionysian) polymorphous perversity. Spinoza's democracy is not representational, but participatory, with the sovereign rights of individuals uncompromised. Spinoza's *conatus*, "the effort by which each thing endeavors to persevere in its being," is a Dionysian unity, of which the "enlightened self interest" of Hobbes and Rousseau are shadowy parodies.

Tom Marshall notes: "This is why Brown uses Christianity and Shakespeare: they are democratic in our world."

NOB: You are like the capitalists, you think that you have to own it, that that gives it power.

DP: The capitalists are right. I call it biblio-osmosis: just having it on the shelf you absorb its vibrations at night while you sleep.

(Nobby handed me back the book and got out of the car. The first challenge was to cross the stream. There was a log that spanned the gulch, the remnant of what had once been a log and plank bridge—this is how I usually crossed. The log was a long way above the creek bed, fifteen or twenty feet, and I enjoyed showing off my balance and nerve. Nobby would usually work his way down the bank and find a way to cross by stepping from rock to rock, using his cane.

This was a long hike with spectacular scenery and some very challenging trail. At several places the trail is washed out, and we would have to climb down into little gullies and ravines, then work our way back up the hillside.

Nobby was eighty-two years old at the time, but I never made any allowances on account of his age, and never offered assistance except where one would do so for any fellow climber. Still, on tricky crossings like this one I usually held my breath until he was safely across. I opened a new thread.)

DP: Do you believe that there are any books so dangerous that they should be restricted, not made available for the general public?[1]

NOB: No, that is against Dionysus. I think Dionysus means demos.[2]

[3] Though Nobby mentioned them in relation to *Life Against Death* more than once, the Weather Underground, of course, didn't appear until 1969. The gist of what he was saying is that he was unprepared for his sudden role as a prophet of the New Left.

[4] I COULD have said no, right then. I didn't. Thus, this ...

[5] "The Holy Lie" and the burden of the privileged classes to protect high culture from the vulgar mob—even if what they are really talking about is tennis or yachting.

The problem, good anarchists explain to us, is not whether the ruler is wise or stupid, but with the ruler as such.

[6] Alfred Edward Taylor, *Plato, the Man and the Work*, 1926.

> *In due course, however, liberal Anglicans such as Sewell and Blackie and A. E. Taylor got hold of Plato and used his doctrines to uphold traditional Christian ethics against utilitarianism— whereupon his [Plato's] university status at once rose appreciably. The utilitarians, in turn, employed Plato's moral and political philosophy as a surrogate to replace Christian values: where Taylor had 'transformed the Republic into a Hellenic Pilgrim's Progress', Grote saw Plato as a kind of radical Benthamite, a questioner of all established values.* (Peter Green, *Classical Bearings*)

See also I. F. Stone, *The Trial of Socrates*, for Plato as an anti-democrat.

DP: But you once said that because of groups like the Weather Underground claiming *Life Against Death* to be part of their theoretical foundation, you decided to write *Love's Body* in a more esoteric, less accessible style.[3]

NOB: Yes, but there is a problem with that. I don't have it all worked out. As you know, my mother was an esotericist, and the elitism in the occult bothers me. Grades of advancement. Degrees.

DP: Adepts.

NOB: That fits precisely. Demos/elite. Aristos/demos: remaining problems. When I am dead and you write about me, begin with that premise.[4]

DP: If there is a problem with elitism in the occult, then there is also a problem in Plato.[5]

NOB: If you would read the book you bought, you would know about that. You will look at Plato differently after Serres. You have to look at the *Symposium*.

DP: I was thinking of the *Republic*.

NOB: I think that the *Symposium* is a palinode, trying to correct the mistakes of the *Republic*.

DP: Was it written after?

NOB: What does the latest scholarship say? Do you have a book on Plato? My book is Taylor, he was a dean at Oxford in the twenties, but a lot of scholarship came out of Germany in the thirties. I don't think Oxford knew what to do, so they just kept Taylor.[6]

DP: (Musing)

[7] Nobby's furthest swing to esotericism is in his Phi Beta Kappa address, where he calls for a return to the mysteries:

> *Mysteries are intrinsically esoteric, and as such are an offense to democracy: is not publicity a democratic principle? Publication makes it republican—a thing of the people. The pristine academies were esoteric and aristocratic, self-consciously separate from the profanely vulgar. Democratic resentment denies that there can be anything that can't be seen by everybody; in the democratic academy truth is subject to public verification; truth is what any fool can see. This is what is meant by the so-called scientific method: so-called science is the attempt to democratize knowledge—the attempt to substitute method for insight, mediocrity for genius, by getting a standard operating procedure.* (A/M 3-4)

Nobby was already falling in love with M. C. Richards when he broke his "vow of silence" to speak at Columbia, and his anthroposophical readings may have contributed to his emphasis on "mysteries." M. C. had sent Brown her poem "Apocalypse." In the same speech Brown makes his first explicit call for a "Dionysian Christianity," of Dionysus as the god who is both "manifest and hidden," and that poetry is "veiled truth," the mode of mysterious transmission.

> *Our real choice is between holy and unholy madness; open your eyes and look around you—madness is in the saddle anyhow. Freud is the measure of our unholy madness, as Nietzsche is the prophet of the holy madness, of Dionysus, the mad truth.* ("Apocalypse, The Place of Mystery in the Life of the Mind," A/M, 2)

Writing about *Closing Time*, David Greenham states:

> Brown thinks that he finds in the poetic logic of The New Science *"a way to transcend Vico's occultist elitism."* (CT 107) However, what Brown in fact finds in Vico is a way of overcoming his own occult elitism and returning the mysteries to the people. (Greenham, *The Resurrection of the Body*, 172)

The bridge, perhaps ironically, is *Finnegans Wake*. >>

NOB: Most important is my Phi Beta Kappa address. You have to look at demos and elitism and the occult.[7]

DP: Demos/Aristos is Athens versus Sparta.

NOB: Sparta is fraternity. See Ortega y Gasset on the sportive origin of the state.[8]

>> [8] The theme of the "Liberty" chapter of *Love's Body*:

According to the current patriarchal orthodoxy, Sparta is a "land-owning aristocracy," and then the great war is between progressive, democratic, and commercial Athens and reactionary, aristocratic, and agrarian Sparta. The truth is that the indispensable basis for a "land-holding aristocracy"—the house-and-land-holding patriarchal family—is lacking at Sparta.... Spartan society was a hierarchy not based on either property or blood, but on graduated degrees of initiation—initiation into secret societies.... One might expect the homosexual emphasis of fraternal organization to degrade the status of women; but it was at Sparta that women had freedom and dignity, while the women of the Athenian patriarchal family were degraded into nonentity. (LB 12-13)

The energy which builds fraternal organization is in rebellion against the family and the father; it is youthful energy. Ortega y Gasset can see that the primeval political association is the secret society, not the gray-bearded senate, because he is willing to acknowledge the youthful, or sportive, or playful origin of the state. "It was not," he says, "the worker, the intellectual, the priest, properly speaking, or the businessman who started the great political process, but youth, preoccupied with women and resolved to fight—the lover, the warrior, the athlete." ... The brothers feel the incest taboo and the lure of strange women; and adopt military organization (gang organization) for purposes of rape. Politics as gang bang. The game is juvenile, or, as Freud would say, infantile; and deadly serious; it is the game of Eros and Thanatos; of sex and war. (LB 14-15)

[9] I had lent Nobby Diamond's *In Search of the Primitive*, but, oddly (I thought), the book hadn't impressed him much.

[10] Any examples of aberrant, criminal behavior among the population are seized upon by the state and their press and their allied intellectuals to support the Hobbesian view of human nature, and to hide the sociopathic and *unnecessary* nature of the state itself. Brown places a small wager on Spinoza:

> *The metaphysics of the* Ethics, *distilled from the historical studies of the* Tractatus Theologico-Politicus, *needs to be translated into a physics of politics, a physics robust enough to overthrow the giant of absolutism, Thomas Hobbes.* (A/M 120)

For Brown, state formation and cannibalism are co-emergent: "The brothers overcame the father, and all partook of his body." (*LB* 164) (Both Actaeon and Pentheus are killed and eaten for *challenging* divine authority, not because of the *absence* of authority.) Through the Eucharist, cannibalism becomes the basis of a Dionysian Christianity:

> *The supper is the last thing, not the cross: eschatology is eating; the marriage feast of the Lamb.* (LB 171)

> *From crucifixion to eating; from the bloody to the bloodless sacrifice; from the old to the new; from the letter to the spirit. Idols require human sacrifice, literally; Moloch. Abstain from things offered to idols, and from blood. The problem of war is the problem of idolatry, or literalism. The crude materialism of physical conquest.... Therefore the opposite of war, the true war, is poetry.* (LB 173)

DP: In Stanley Diamond's critique of progress, he defines civilization as a culture based on hierarchy, imperialism, writing, taxation, and standing armies.[9]

NOB: You are making the state satanic. To what end?

DP: That people are by nature cooperative, as in Kropotkin and anthropology. That the big question is the argument with Hobbes and Freud, on what is human nature. They say that without a police force we'd be eating each other.[10]

NOB: That means taking the *Republic* & *Laws*, which is what they teach in English "public school." They don't teach the *Symposium*.

DP: Gary [Snyder] characterized the emergence of the state in China as a giant protection racket. A group of armed riders show up and say "pay us, or something bad will happen to you."

(The trail had been leading downstream through brush and chaparral, gradually wending its way out of the river canyon. At two places there were down redwood trees that we either had to clamber over or find a way around. At several places the brush was thick and we had to punch our way through buck brush and mountain lilac.)

NOB: What have you been reading?

DP: *King Lear*. And watching video recordings of *Lear*: Scofield. And Olivier.

NOB: What led to *Lear*?

DP: (Thinking)

NOB: Not answering? What, do you see yourself as Lear with your daughter? Is she Cordelia, or Regan?

DP: Cordelia.

NOB: But what are you looking for, how did it start?

DP: The Fool, I think. The Fool is the key to the play.

[11] *FW* 463

[12] Actually, the quote is Lear's statement to the storm, before he enters the hovel and sees Poor Tom. Nobby gets it right.

[13] We have all neglected this. "Truth comes riding a donkey." (*LB* 238)

[14] Pound, "Canto LXXXI."

NOB: The play is a comedy, that's why the Fool is the key. Shakespeare shows how tragedy is comedy. Dionysus is comedy. You have to look for it in comedy.

DP: But isn't Dionysus the god of the tragedians? The *Birth of Tragedy* ...

NOB: I don't believe that. Dionysus is always laughing:

> Got by one goat, suckled by the same nanna,
> one twitch, one nature makes us oldworld kin.[11]

(The trail emerged from the brush to an open meadow. A sharp wind was blowing and we both thought of the heath.)

NOB: He questions nothing ... He can't accept it.

DP: "Nothing will come of nothing."

NOB: Nothing will come of nothing. I think that is the key to the play. It could be called "much ado about nothing."

DP: Demos ... Lear comes to that on the heath, seeing Edgar.

NOB: No, not Edgar.

DP: Yes, he has questioned the elements, and called them vile servants. Then he sees the naked Poor Tom. Pomp, take physick.[12]

NOB: Take physick, pomp. I have neglected this.[13]

DP: *Pull down thy vanity,*
Paquin, pull down.
the green casque has outdone your elegance.[14]

(Nobby seemed to take the Pound quote for granted: he merely nodded and continued his thread.)

NOB: I haven't gotten to Shakespeare. I think it's in Milton. And *Lycidus* is the best.

[15] Christopher Hill, *Milton and the English Revolution*.

[16] "Chance has its reasons."

[17] Logos: a used bookstore in Santa Cruz. We were both regulars.

[18] Keats, "On Sitting Down to Read King Lear Once Again":

The bitter-sweet of this Shakespearian fruit.

Nobby was "on," as they say.

> *Fame is no plant that grows on mortal soil,*
> *Nor in the glistering foil*
> *Set off to the world, nor in broad rumour lies,*
> *But lives and spreads aloft by those pure eyes*
> *And perfect witness of all-judging Jove;*
> *As he pronounces lastly on each deed,*
> *Of so much fame in heaven expect thy meed.*

(Now it was my turn to nod. Nobby continued.)

> NOB: And it is in the first edition, or maybe the second edition, of *Lycidus*, where he has that quote from Petronius.
>
> *Si recte calculas ulrique naufragium est.*

(I looked at him and waited for his translation.)

> NOB: "If you calculate correctly, there is shipwreck everywhere." Christopher Hill used it as the motto for his book on Milton.[15]

(This was a moment I was prepared for.)

> DP: I have another quote from Petronius: *Suam habet fortuna rationem.*[16]

(This earned me an approving look and nod, and Nobby jotted down the line. As for chance, we had gone over that ground so many times in our walks that neither of us was inclined to reopen that discussion just yet, and we walked in silence for awhile.)

> NOB: I've bought a number of the Arden Shakespeare's recently at Logos.[17]
>
> DP: I thought you said it was in Milton.
>
> NOB: (With a smile) But I had thought that I would come to Shakespeare at the end of my life.
>
> > *When through the old oak forest I am gone,*
> > *Let me not wander in a barren dream,*
> > *But when I am consumed in the fire,*
> > *Give me new Phoenix wings to fly at my desire.*[18]

[19] Robinson Jeffers, "Bixby's Landing," *Cawdor*, 1928.

[20] Andrew Marvell, "The Garden," one of Nobby's favorites. E. R. Dodds comments on Euripides' strophe from *Bacchae* (866-867), "*Like a fawn at play in the green joy of a meadow when it has escaped the frightening hunt*": "'Green joy,' a colour-word applied to an abstract noun, is bold for a Greek poet, though not so bold as Marvell ... χλοεραῖς λείμακος ἡδοναῖς has perhaps the effect of a compound, 'green-meadow-joy.'"

[21] *Viriditas*, Hildegard von Bingham's word, for whom Jesus was Greenness Incarnate.

[22] Naomi Goldenberg, in a feminist critique of Brown ("Reviewing a Mentor: The Concept of Body in the Work of Norman O. Brown," *Returning Words to Flesh: Feminism, Psychoanalysis, and the Resurrection of the Body*), states: "In *Life Against Death* it is important to understand that Brown is, in fact, talking about the resurrection of only one type of body: a male body, and a particular male body at that." What she seems to mean by this is that Brown's unrepressed man, being freed from guilt, anxiety, and "unconscious oral, anal, and genital fantasies of return to the maternal womb," is no body at all other than a dead one—certainly not a female body that menstruates, gives birth, or goes through menopause. Goldenberg states: "Instead of resurrecting the perfect, above-it-all male body, which is, after all, the dead, 'touch-me-not-for-I-am-newly-risen body' of the New Testament, I suggest that there are better bodies to resurrect." Goldenberg suggests, no surprise, a maternal body, which she goes on to say is more the case in *Love's Body*. (As an aside, note that when Brown wrote to M. C. Richards to end their affair, his "Latin exit," as Richards characterized it, was "*noli me tangere*".)

Goldenberg continues her critique by suggesting that in *Love's Body*, Brown is unable to maintain the poignancy of desire and imperfection urged by his words "Admit the void, accept loss forever.... Wisdom is mourning; blessed are they that mourn." Instead Brown seeks the apocalypse, the body and the world consumed by fire. (Marcuse, in "Love Mystified" makes this same point—that, in the end, Brown's "body" is spiritual, not carnal.)

DP: What is YOUR favorite Shakespeare?

NOB: Keats has a letter on that subject ...

DP: And?

NOB: Right now, I'm liking *The Tempest*.

DP: Have you seen the John Gielgud movie?

(More discussion followed, the erotic element in The Tempest. *We walked further until we came to the end of the grassy vale and the ruins of an old lime kiln. There was a metal arch for a gate to what might have been an old carriage house. It all could have been temple ruins. Nobby had been showing off the lion's share of the quotes so far, so I tried some Jeffers.)*

DP: Wine-hearted solitude,
our mother the wilderness,
Men's failures are often as beautiful
as men's triumphs, but your returnings
Are even more precious than your
first presence.[19]

NOB: That's beautiful. Is that Jeffers? Please send that to me.

(Nobby took a few steps, adding a capping couplet from Marvell.)

NOB: Annihilating all that's made
To a green thought in a green shade.[20]

DP: *Viriditas*. The greenness is all.[21]

(We were at a locked metal gate with a prominent "NO TRESPASSING" sign. Nobby hung his cane on the top of the gate and clambered over. I followed him.)

NOB: There are mistakes in *Love's Body*, it's too Christian.[22]

23 I'm afraid we both enjoyed abuse. A friend, when I related this conversation to her, thought this remark cruel. But there was nothing about Nobby that was dying—at the end of hikes such as this, I was the one who was worn out, not Nobby. I was commenting on Nobby's morbidity, and it was entirely within the abusive guidelines that Nobby himself had established for our exchanges.

24 "Fear of death disturbs me," in William Dunbar's "Lament for the Makers." See also Kenneth Rexroth, "Thou Shalt Not Kill."

25 Now my father was Lear, and I was challenged to be Cordelia.

26 In *Hermes the Thief*, Brown distinguishes robbery (ἁρπαγή) by force (βία) from theft (κλοπή) by stealth (δόλος), and concludes that the epithet of the god came from being a trickster, the god whose gift was stealth and cunning and deceit, rather than from his youthful robbery of Apollo's cattle. To the early Greeks (as to the Indo-Europeans generally), cattle raiding was armed robbery, a socially approved pursuit, while theft by stealth or tricky deals, mercantile acquisitiveness, was, to Hesiod, an affront to the gods.

Brown completed his "high career" from Hermes to Dionysus by reconnecting with Hermes in the last essay of his last book, "Dionysus in 1990":

> *Capitalism has proven itself more dynamic—i.e., Dionysian—than socialism. Its essential nature is to be out of control: exuberant energy, exploiting every opportunity, to extract a surplus.* (*A/M* 189)

DP: If a dying man in his last days wants to spend his time composing a palinode, I won't say it's wrong.[23]

NOB: You must deliver a palinode yourself, on drugs. I always rejected them.

(We took a couple of steps, and then Nobby decided that he'd better retreat from this facile assumption of moral superiority before I organized my counterattack.)

NOB: Well, not entirely. There was alcohol. I was at Wesleyan, and it wasn't allowed there.

DP: Thank you. *Timor mortis conturbat me.*[24]

(Nobby went on to tell stories about the official and unofficial lifestyles at Wesleyan, and how he had had to hide his drinking.)

DP: My father was anti-alcohol, rabidly. We were having a family dinner once, at a restaurant, and the waiter started out by asking if we'd like to order drinks. After the waiter had left my father muttered that he wasn't going to leave that waiter a tip.

NOB: It can be so important: this nothing.

DP: Excellent. Thank you.[25]

(Ahead of us a dozen cows were grazing. They were on both sides of the trail, so we had no choice but to walk right through them. Nobby was visibly nervous.)

NOB: Isn't there a chapter in *Ulysses* called "Cattle of the Sun"?

DP: There should be. I thought it was in NOB, *Hermes the Thief.*[26]

NOB: I wrote *Hermes the Thief* as my dissertation at Wisconsin. I went to Wisconsin because A. D. Winspear was there. He was a Marxist classicist. I was going to write about Dionysus. I'm very glad that I didn't, I would have gotten it all wrong. I was going to use Dionysus as a maritime commerce symbol. Aphrodite also.

²⁷ NOB would never give me the pleasure of admiring any of my attempts at magical realism. In fact, such attempts seemed to bother him. Nobby's reality was in books and ideas, and trying to mix that up with the world of things, to instantiate the mythic into the phenomenal, seemed like a transgression of the reality principle—in spite of many of his own dicta, such as:

> *The goal cannot be the elimination of magical thinking, or madness; the goal can only be conscious magic, or conscious madness; conscious mastery of these fires. And dreaming while awake.* (LB 254)

DP: She WAS beloved of mariners ...

(We passed through the cattle. I had a chance to tell my cow dream.)

DP: You know, all these cattle were once men. Conceited men. Well, maybe not so much that they were conceited, but just that they were brilliant. They had wonderful ideas, at least they thought so. Their ideas were so wonderful and fascinating that they became absorbed in them, in their own ideas. Until, after a while, that was all they ever thought about, and gradually their heads dropped to the ground. Finally, when they got hungry, they just began eating grass, like Nebuchadnezzar, so they wouldn't have to interrupt their thoughts.

NOB: (Somewhat mystified) These cattle here?

DP: Oh yes, look at their faces.

NOB: I don't see anything.[27]

DP: I've been reading Cabeza de Vaca.

NOB: Why are you reading that? What is it?

DP: Nunez Cabeza de Vaca was the first European to walk through the interior of North America. He was shipwrecked with two companions and captured by Indians, who took everything he had and made him a slave. At one point he was asked to perform a healing for a sick child. Nunez prayed to the Savior and the child was healed.

After that he wandered for eight years as a naked ascetic, living, as he thought, like Jesus, and selflessly praying to God and Christ to heal the sick everywhere he went. The Indians traded him from tribe to tribe and he and his two companions became famous healers.

One day, when they had been traded south into what is now Mexico, the Indians brought him men and women with terrible gunshot and sword wounds, and

stories about fearsome men who slaughtered them and took them away as captives. It turned out to be the Spanish, and Nunez was horrified to find out that the Church was involved in the slavery and the killing.

NOB: Do you ever tell stories like that to your father?

DP: Yes.

NOB: Does he say, oh, that was the Catholics, not the Methodists?

DP: Yes.

NOB: (Reflecting) You've had a hard life.

DP: Yes.

NOB: (Very amused) You're not going to deny it?

DP: No.

NOB: The last thing I wrote on the Spanish Conquest was my essay about Juana de la Cruz.

DP: Hmmm, there was another essay on Juana de la Cruz ...

NOB: Paz.

DP: Someone else. Graves, I think.

NOB: In what context?

DP: Let's see ... The Muse, Graves' "Muse Theory." The Muse is a woman so most poets are men. So he looks for the exceptions and has a theory about what it takes for a woman to do it, and he looks at Juana de la Cruz. Yes. So it must be Graves.

NOB: How could you remember such a thing!

(After perhaps half a mile the trail curved back toward open meadows. There was another barbed wire fence to contend with. The property owners were evidently more serious about keeping people out at this gate than at the previous gate, because there was extra barbed wire strung over the top

[28] "Daphne, or Metamorphosis," NOB's hymn to Renunciation. (NOB might have called it "sublimation.")

The reconciliation of spirit and nature; the opposition of sexuality and sublimation overcome. When our eyes are opened, we perceive that in sexuality the object is not the literal girl; but the symbolic girl, the tree. It is always something else that we want. The object is always transcendent. (A/M 19)

[29] I didn't know it at the time, but loss of smell is one of the first indications of Alzheimer's.

[30] Andrew Marvell, "The Garden," one of Nobby's favorites.

of the gate, and around the sides of the posts to which the gate was chained. Sometimes we climbed over the barbed wire, sometimes I would find a stretch of fence where I could press down on the middle or bottom wire with my foot and pull up on the wire above it so that Nobby could climb through, then pass through myself when Nobby held them for me. Sometimes we would climb over at a place where a young buckeye tree had grown up on the fence line. A sign said: "VIOLATORS WILL BE PROSECUTED.")

> NOB: I cannot remember my father at all. It's just a blank. I can't see his contribution to this. Now my mother is a different story. Did I tell you what she had carved into the headboard of her marriage bed?
>
> DP: No.
>
> NOB: "Near, very near, to Paradise, is renunciation."

(I had nothing to say to this, I just kept walking, absorbing what he had said. Over the crest of the hill the trail turned back into the forest, mostly oak, bay, and madrone, with a few second growth redwoods in the canyons. A large bay tree had fallen across a gulley. It was still partially rooted, and branches had sprouted along its length, growing straight up as new trunks. Some of them were already over ten feet high. We stopped to look at it.)

> NOB: What is that?
>
> DP: It's the Resurrection.
>
> NOB: I don't mean that, what kind of tree is it?
>
> DP: Bay Laurel, your Daphne.[28]
>
> NOB: This tree? How can you tell?
>
> DP: (Crushes a leaf) Smell it.
>
> NOB: (Shakes his head) I can't smell.[29]
>
> DP: C'mon, this is immortality.
>
> NOB: Casting the body's vest aside,
>   My soul into the boughs does glide.[30]

(I was about to quote some of the Marvell back to him: "The gods, that mortal beauty chase, Still in a tree did end their race," but Nobby jumped ahead.)

NOB: What does your daughter know about your father's theology?

DP: Quite a bit. She has spent a lot of time with him.

NOB: (Twisting the knife once again) Does she know about your Oedipal history with it?

DP: You keep saying that. You think it's Oedipal?

NOB: Oh my yes!

(We had reached a place with some shade, overlooking the fields and headlands north of Santa Cruz, and paused to catch our breath.)

DP: I admit, a couple of recent dreams have made a small crack in my skepticism of such matters.

NOB: A dream about your father?

DP: Yes, and one about my mother, just the other night. In the dream about my father I was fighting with him. He was pushing me back and I was trying to fight him off but my arms were too small and weak. He pushed me down into a corner and then I found the power of the word. I said: "It's *you* who have the alcohol problem! You are the alcoholic here, and you're trying to push your disease onto everyone else." That pushed him back.

NOB: He had his arms on you?

DP: Yes, but he was stronger than I was until I found the words.

NOB: (Thinks) I'm not sure how to interpret that.

DP: And my mother was there. After I had pushed my father off with my words, I glanced over at her, and she was torn between her loves: she was proud of me but she wouldn't, or couldn't, show it.

(*A red-tailed hawk circled above us. The soaproot was in flower, but it was still too early in the afternoon for the vespertine flowers to be fully open, and we resumed walking.*)

DP: The dream about my mother I just had the other night. My friend Susan was in the dream too. In the dream my mother was young. My mother had just hugged me and told me to be careful or something like that, then she started dry-humping me.

NOB: What?

DP: You know, like this (wiggles hips). So I looked over to Susan and said "C'mon now, I don't have any problem with an Oedipus complex."

NOB: (Laughs) At my age my dreams have lost a lot of color.

(*I was about to quip that he should take some drugs, but kept quiet.*)

NOB: Four years ago I kept a notebook and would record some of my dreams, but not now ...

DP: Some of them I don't think you want to write down. I think it fixes them, stops them from moving and working.

NOB: Yes, maybe so. I had a graduate student who had four thousand dreams recorded. But I don't think you can really record a dream. It can't be written.

DP: I distrust writing dreams, except for a few special ones.

NOB: Freud had a rather complete trust in the literal recording of dreams.

DP: The letter killeth. I think it has to be a mnemonic piece, something that evokes and brings the dream back to mind.

NOB: That says something about style.

[31] George Hitchcock, the poet, playwright, and painter who taught at UCSC (Porter College) for nineteen years. Hitchcock edited the poetry journal *Kayak*, which he published from 1964 to 1984.

[32] In "Love Hath Reason, Reason None," Brown states that Marcuse's critique of *Love's Body* was right, that Chapter XII, "Resurrection," is "too Christian," and that the problem has to do with the apocalyptic sense of newness, his quest to demand from psychoanalysis a Christian sense of renewal:

> *Archetypal patterns of eternal recurrence discovered in psychoanalysis are identified with theological patterns of redemptive history (Christ as the second Adam, etc.). By this path the conclusion is reached that "There is another kind of Protestantism possible, a Dionysian Christianity"—the final destination to which Marcuse objected.* (LHR 220)

"Dionysian Christianity," an "ecstatic disaffiliation to be achieved by extraordinary feats of vision," is linked to "symbolic consciousness," which is linked to "'eternity' (as in Blake), identified with 'eternal recurrence' (as in Nietzsche), and with the repetition-compulsion (as in Freud)." After excusing himself as being under the influence of "the American counter-culture of the period," Brown places his new wager on chance as another kind of newness:

> *It contradicts both the Christian idea of eternity and the Nietzschean idea of eternal recurrence.* (LHR 220)

[33] *Augustine does entertain the objection that the happiness of the saints in heaven, which has to be unalloyed, will be spoilt by the thought of the others—mothers, fathers, sisters, brothers, lovers—being tortured in Hell. Augustine, no man to flee from paradox, answers that the saints in Heaven will enjoy the torments of the wicked in Hell, because of course they love justice.* (*LHR* 217)

[34] In Lucretius, the "swerve" keeps atoms from all falling to the ground. Here the *clinamen* implies the presence of inclination, or affinity. And spontaneous behavior.

The *clinamen* is an integral part of the thought of Michel Serres, especially in *The Birth of Physics*.

DP: Gary pointed out to me that Ovid named all of Actaeon's dogs.

NOB: He not only named them, he embellished, giving each one's pedigree, but it doesn't come off well: it's too mannered.

(We talked more about style, which led to surrealism. I mentioned George Hitchcock.[31] NOB said he wouldn't have thought of Hitchcock, that he was thinking of painters, Dali. We talked about Hitchcock for a while, then quieted as we reached a long open climb.)

NOB: That paper you have ("Love Hath Reason") is wrong.[32]

DP: Is there a new edition?

NOB: No, I will pass into the beyond with no new edition.

DP: I liked the quote from Augustine, about justice.[33]

NOB: Justice won't do, therefore Christianity won't do.

DP: Do you know that poem, "The Deepest Sensuality," by D. H. Lawrence?

NOB: No.

DP: The profoundest of all sensualities
　　　is the sense of truth.
　　　And the next deepest sensual experience
　　　is the sense of justice.

"Next deepest" is an understatement, I've always thought.

NOB: We must throw out justice, along with causality.

DP: I'm uneasy about throwing out causality along with justice.

NOB: Chance means that there is no pre-ordained order.

DP: But you will still admit the *clinamen*?[34]

35 Because of the *clinamen*, behavior is indeterminate. Serres (*Hermes: Literature, Science, Philosophy*) and Ilya Prigonine ("Postface," in same) introduce this idea within the turbulence in a laminar flow. (Serres goes on to connect the "V" of the *clinamen* to Venus.) The ultimate ontological status of chance becomes irrelevant. As does Freudian determinism.

36 *Meaning is not in things but in between; in the iridescence, the interplay; in the interconnections; at the intersections, at the crossroads. Meaning is transitional as it is transitory; in the puns or bridges, the correspondence.* (LB 247)

37 But there is a clue in Blake's poem, "To Nobodaddy":

Why dost thou hide thyself in clouds
From every searching Eye

As the *clinamen* is hidden in turbulence, meaning is mercurial and hidden in the dynamics of continuous creation: grasp it, and it's gone.

38 Cf., however,

Christian typology; karmic reincarnation; the phylogenetic factor in psychoanalysis. The thing that "happened long ago" did not happen to you individually, but to the race archetypically; or, if you prefer, it happened to you "in a previous incarnation." (LB 208)

NOB: Yes, that admits the irrational, and chance.[35]

DP: So even with chance, there is still affinity, yes?

NOB: (Nodded very slightly, kept walking)

DP: I'd say that affinity lets in the *Tao*, the "mysterious female."

(I was feeling a little like an Indian dodging from tree to tree, trying to fight off the cavalry.)

DP: Does chance kill determinism, or is chance the poison that dulls our perceptions of connectedness, that dulls our belief?

NOB: Doubt and belief must be reconciled.[36]

(I could tell that Nobby didn't like the way the discussion was going. For him, the clinamen *was a perturbation, a swerve OUT of the Way. In* Tao *he sensed Meaning, and "Nobodaddy." I tried a different tack.[37])*

DP: On the oldest tarot cards, Justice is blindfolded.

NOB: Is that true?

DP: Yes, so there can still be causality without judgment. Buddhism has karma but not judgment. There's no Last Judgment or eternal damnation in Buddhism.

NOB: Buddhism brings justice back in through reincarnation. Buddhism won't do.[38]

DP: Reincarnation isn't justice, it's cause and effect.

NOB: I don't think you can deny it. You are poor or rich in this life because of what you did in your last life. Buddhism won't do.

DP: (Getting desperate) But you are taking your Buddhism from Asian folk beliefs, and your Christianity from Augustine. That's not fair.

NOB: (Didn't answer, but seemed to accept the point)

[39] I had one chance and one chance only. I chose the *Vimalakirti Sutra* because of its playful style and its descriptions of the transcendence of ordinary morality by bodhisattva action. In the years since, I've often second-guessed myself, wondering if the *Diamond Sutra*—more overtly addressing the philosophy of emptiness—might have been better. Or the *Platform Sutra*, the story of Hui Neng. Nobby owned D. T. Suzuki's book on the *Lankavatara*, but his marginalia didn't extend past Suzuki's introduction.

DP: You should read one real sutra before you throw out Buddhism.

NOB: What should I read?

DP: Vimalakirti. I will lend it you.[39]

NOB: Okay, I will read it. But that doesn't get you off the hook on justice and reincarnation.

DP: You're right. From now on I'm going to be a non-Buddhist Buddhist.

(We hiked over the crest dividing the watershed. The view was spectacular, the land sloping down to the coast, the ocean blue and wide, a mile or two below us. We talked about arranging for a hike down to the ocean—leaving a car or connecting with the bus, but we never did it.

Here we left the trail and hiked northward, cutting horizontally somewhat below the ridge. We passed several small groves of live oak. Beyond the second grove of live oak there was a flat area, somewhat protected from the wind and offering a panoramic view of the coast. Because of the great curve of the Monterey Bay, the Ventana Range behind Big Sur appeared to rise out of the ocean like distant islands on the horizon. This was the extremity of the hike and we sat down on the grass and rested in the shade. Two red-tails soared in the sky. I picked up a stick and drew a circle in the dirt.)

DP: This is Dionysian history, eternal return.

(Then I drew a short vertical line.)

DP: This is Christian history, and if we make it into an arrow, we have the scales of justice.

(I drew the arrow on the top. Nobby was watching with interest.)

DP: So Justice is also the Eon, the Last Judgment, apocalypse.

NOB: I don't understand why you don't get lost in your ideas.

40 The vertical arrow is also tau, the cross, so Eternal Life = Dionysus + Christ: Nobby's whole project.

41 Also, moderation = justice (Aristotle's golden mean); linking geometry, temperance, and the sword of justice through the right triangle.

> [Aristotle] had observed legal justice seated in the spirit of the sovereign civil power and dictating prudence in the senate, fortitude in the armies, and temperance at festivals, as well as the two forms of particular justice: distributive justice in the public treasuries and commutative justice for the most part in the forum; the latter employing arithmetical proportion and the former geometrical. (Vico, *New Science*, sec. 1042)

42 On the other hand, Pascal was an excellent geometer, strictly compass and straight edge, while Descartes' great accomplishment was to QUANTIFY geometry.

Or, we could have chased the ankh to Egypt, the laying out of property lines after the flooding of the Nile. Or we could have gone to Pythagoras, and thus to Plato (Ideas), and thus to grammar and the nature of formal systems. Nobby's equation of geometry and justice was also a jab at Jung (and Rationalism/Thomism in general).

43 Today I would retract my assertion about the relative mathematical abilities of the two philosophers, but not that as to their accomplishments.

> On the mathematical side Pascal is perhaps the greatest might-have-been in history ... a highly gifted mathematician who let his masochistic proclivities for self-torturing and profitless speculations on the sectarian controversies of his day degrade him to what would now be called a religious neurotic. (E. T. Bell, *Men of Mathematics*)

44 Pascal, *Pensees*, III, 206, "On the Necessity of the Wager."

45 *The world is a veil we spin to hide the world.* (LB 261)

(I took that as a compliment, gazed at my drawing for awhile, then drew an ankh.)

    DP: But look here, if we combine them, we get eternal life. The ankh is really just a cross, so Christ = Dionysus + Justice.[40]

$$\mathrm{\circlearrowleft} + \uparrow = \phi$$

(Nobby thought for awhile. I could see that he was a little bothered.)

    NOB: Geometry equals Justice.[41]

    DP: Then what are numbers?

    NOB: Anal.

(After a while we got up and started the long walk back. There were a lot of directions this could go. I thought of Descartes versus Pascal, where Pascal is numbers and Descartes geometry.[42] I tried something I thought would be provocative.)

    DP: Descartes was a greater mathematician than Pascal.

    NOB: How so?

    DP: He married geometry and algebra. Much more important than Pascal's probability work.[43]

    NOB: You think so?

    DP: Oh yes.

    NOB: (Laughs) Weren't you going to find me something on Pascal?

    DP: *The eternal silence of these infinite spaces fills me with dread.*[44]

    NOB: How do you see that?

    DP: It's the "eternity creeps," the fear of chaos and emptiness that makes us cling to systems, or materialism. Or to God.[45]

⁴⁶ Has anyone ever graphed the statistical prevalence of hemorrhoids against religious affiliation? *LAD* suggests there might be more hemorrhoids among Protestants, particularly Lutherans. Perhaps we have here a testable hypothesis as to whether or not Freud's system of psychology is biological.

⁴⁷ In *The Parasite*, Serres begins with Aesop's story of the city rat and the country rat, whose meal is interrupted by the cat.

> *Who, then, is the real interrupter? It is the country rat. Broken himself by the interruptions, these uneasy feelings, the disruptions of his relaxing meal, it is he who definitely breaks the system. He could live on simple and easy chains, but he is horrified by the complex. He does not understand that chance, risk, anxiety, and even disorder can consolidate a system. He trusts only simple, rough, causal relations; he believes that disorder always destroys order. He is a rationalist, the kind we just spoke of. How many of these rough political rats are there around us? How many of them break things they don't understand? How many of these rats simplify? How many of them have built such homogenous, cruel systems upon the horror of disorder and noise?* (Serres, *The Parasite*, 14)

The interrupter is noise, or static, the parasite: the *clinamen*. (It is also Hermes, the god of the crossroads whom Maxwell made into a demon.) Serres also connects the interrupter with the Paraclete, the Holy Ghost (the Third Person).

⁴⁸ Here Nobby might have said, "Yes, or Atalanta," or, "Adonis." Or how about "boar, bore, boorish: a skeptical reductionist on a rampage, sacrificed to Demeter. Or Diarmid, killed by Finn MacCool." That's certainly the way I would write the story. But Nobby rarely played that way. From a text, yes, he was quick to find any mythic resonance, but not from passing events of the phenomenal world. Well, except for Freud, which he perhaps considered "scientific" or "true" in a way that myth was not. In spite of his playfulness on the page, in an open field there was a difference between theory and practice.

NOB: *Timor mortis conturbat me.*

DP: Pascal's work on chance had to do with gambling.

NOB: I've never gambled.

DP: Never?

NOB: No.

DP: But chance begins with gambling. It started with correspondence between Pascal and Fermat. An aristocrat gambler wanted to know how to divide the stakes in a game of dice.

NOB: Money is shit. You know I established that in *Life Against Death.*

(When I didn't answer, Nobby made another reference to "filthy lucre," but I was thinking about other possibilities, following up on the dice thread, such as "and thus, the electron." John Cage was another possibility, of course. Now we were at hoarding, which we could have related to Pascal's fear of emptiness, or to the "hungry ghosts," the Buddhist pretas, whom we have most unwisely incarnated at the center of our society as corporations. Or we could have gone to shit as pollution, or to shit as poison and then to my own "poison path" formulations. Or, ironically, I could have said "so chance is anal."[46]

As it happened, the meal was interrupted.[47] We had just hiked over a saddle down into some grassy oaklands, and were surrounded by the devastation from the rooting of wild pigs. I couldn't see them, but I could hear them. They were close. Nobby was nervous and looked alarmed. I still had the stick that I had picked up and felt reckless enough to go after them. I ran around in a big circle to try to get a glimpse of the pigs, but didn't see any of them.)

DP: Circe is near.[48]

(I told Nobby that feral pigs were an ecological problem, and for effect, added a few remarks on the deliciousness of acorn-fed pork. But we didn't linger.)

[49] It was as if asking "what really happened, historically" had no meaning. What "really" happened is what is in the myths and the scholarly books.

> ... there is a distinction between "what actually happened," events as seen by the eye of historical materialism, and "what is really going on," events sub specie aeternitatis, as seen by the inward, clairvoyant eye, the second sight. (A/M 80)

[50] What's involved is the Orphic revision that made Dionysianism into a salvation religion:

> The Orphics changed Dionysos [Dionysus] himself by emphasizing his role as the lord who conquers death. Although certain myths from Greece and elsewhere had depicted Dionysos as the one who returns from the dead, such a belief was not of overriding importance in the mainstream of Greek Dionysian religion in the earlier, classical era. Later, Orphics made Dionysos' return from the dead the central motif of their religion....

> Orphism changed the purpose of religion from the collective celebration of the joys of life to purification of the soul, introduced the principle of the priority of written scripture as the defining trait of religion, and greatly reduced the leadership role of women. Orphism also anticipated the myth of original sin in its notion that all human beings were descended from the violence-prone Titans. (Arthur Evans, *The God of Ecstasy*, 158-159)

Heraclitus stated that Dionysus and Hades were one and the same.

[51] Walter F. Otto, *Dionysus: Myth and Cult*. Marcel Detienne, *Dionysos Slain*, and *Dionysos at Large*.

DP: So what about those stories about Artemis, *the Golden Bough*, and the self-castration, did that really happen?

NOB: (Confused) What do you mean?

DP: I mean, is there historical attestation, apart from the myths?[49]

(Nobby demurred several times. Something about my question wasn't connecting—something about my attempt to differentiate the myths and stories from "actual" history. I got the feeling that I was committing a transgression. I wasn't sure if he was just going to keep silent or hit me with his cane. With great reluctance, Nobby mentioned a particular temple where the priests castrated themselves. From there we speculated on the theory that the so-called "breasts" covering the Diana of Ephesus were really bull's testicles.)

DP: So are the stories of *omaphagia* in the Dionysian rites Christian propaganda?

NOB: No! Don't let your Christian tendencies pollute the true religion.

(We retraced our steps back to the barbed wire fence, stretched the wires as much as we could, and crawled though.)

DP: Why is Dionysus on so many sarcophagi, instead of, say, Persephone?[50]

NOB: I have to think about that.

DP: What about Otto and Detienne?[51]

NOB: There is nothing new for NOB in Otto or Detienne.

DP: Was Otto off base by insisting on the Grecian origin of Dionysus?

NOB: He was a Nazi. It was important to him for Dionysus to be Greek.

⁵² Actually, I had jumped over India and was thinking of the mythical fox girls in Japan, but we never got to that.

⁵³ Sanskrit root *bhaj*, to divide, share, allocate; hence Skt. *bhakti*, to love, worship, revere, perhaps through the sharing of food as devotional religion (one meaning of Skt. *bhaktá*, which through the phonological shift $bh \rightarrow f$ is Greek φαγειν, to eat, devour). *Omaphagia*, then, would be the sharing of the raw liver before cooking the meat.

Perhaps related is *Bakis*, the nympholeptic soothsayer and keeper of a nymph's shrine. See Jennifer Larson, *Greek Nymphs*.

⁵⁴ *Bagaios* was a title of the Phrygian Zeus.

DP: Do you think that Dionysus changes sex going east?

NOB: Why do you ask?

DP: A couple of books I've been reading. Arthur Evans, *The God of Ecstasy*, and Alain Danielou, *Shiva and Dionysus*.[52]

NOB: Alain Danielou, yes, he's interesting. His brother is Cardinal Danielou.

DP: Danielou claims that "Bakchos" and "Bakhta" are cognate.[53]

NOB: He might be right. It would have to come through Phrygian, I think. What do the linguists say?[54]

DP: Nobody really knows. It doesn't follow the regular phonological shift, so it would have to be a loan word.

NOB: That would follow.

(The trail flattened out again and curved into the forest. A naked and strikingly beautiful Indian girl suddenly appeared out of the trees and walked nonchalantly along the trail about forty feet in front of us. I call her an "Indian" girl because her sole apparel was a feather that she had tied into her long braid. She looked as good from the back as she had from the front. Neither of us commented on the sudden apparition.)

DP: Danielou builds a case for the identity of Dionysus and Shiva. They're both naked gods, they both are connected to the bull, and the rites are so similar that Alexander's soldiers recognized Shiva as Dionysus when they got to India.

NOB: Alexander thought he was being Dionysus when he invaded India.

DP: Except that Dionysus's weapons were tambourines. And most of his soldiers were women.

55 Such is honor among thieves. The "affair" evidently remained platonic (or nearly so), despite M. C.'s efforts to the contrary. I have been unable to find any reference to the dream in Richard's papers at the Getty Museum, though my search was not exhaustive. Also, there are a large number of boxes of Richard's papers still privately held and not yet fully catalogued.

56 Donne, "The Ecstasy." The last stanza goes:

> *And if some lover, such as we,*
> > *Have heard this Dialogue of One,*
> *Let him still mark us, he shall see*
> > *Small change, when we are to bodies gone.*

57 See note in Dodds, *Bacchae*, 78.

58 More good advice I've clearly ignored. See my *Inspired Madness: The Gifts of Burning Man*.

NOB: The second half of *Love's Body* is about Dionysus. *Love's Body* wasn't the original title. The title is from John Donne. The inspiration came from a dream of a woman with whom I was having an affair. You must never reveal this.[55]

> To our bodies turn we then, that so
> Weak men on love reveal'd may look;
> Love's mysteries in souls do grow,
> But yet the body is his book:[56]

(I just kept walking, letting Nobby's revelation sink in, and waiting to see if he would say more. The naked woman was continuing her casual walk along the trail in front of us. I kept thinking of Phryne.)

DP: Did the queen of Athens really have sex with Dionysus?

NOB: It was an important part of the *Anthesteria*. Do you know where they performed the rite?

DP: I think so.

NOB: The building was called the "Bull House."

DP: Soma was placed in the thigh of Indra, like Dionysus was placed into the thigh of Zeus, so we could say that the penis becomes a womb.[57]

NOB: Don't use that! It has "NOB" written all over it.

DP: So, if you died I could claim it as a newly discovered unpublished manuscript of NOB.

NOB: (Laughs) Dionysus is a shorthand for me. You shouldn't use it—it's grounds for dismissal.[58] It's all too archaic. I mean nobody is going to bow down and worship Dionysus.

DP: Alas, alas.

(The naked girl turned off the trail, and disappeared into the trees.)

[59] John L. Brooke, *The Refiner's Fire: The Making of Mormon Cosmology, 1644-1844*.

[60] Nobby was also reading *The Burned-Over District: The Social and Intellectual History of Enthusiastic Religion in Western New York, 1800-1850*, by Whitney R. Cross, which he admired and considered a model of good scholarship, not only in content, but in style and tone. He was fascinated by the contradictions in ultraism between individual inspiration versus crowd psychology, and between collective enthusiasm versus thoughtful individuality, moderation, and rationality. Nobby sent me a number of quotes from the book that he said specifically related to (1) Dionysus versus Christ; (2) John Cage; (3) NOB's "Apocalypse 1960," "Dionysus in 1990," and "Love Hath Reason"; and (4) the counterculture in America 1960-1990. I think Nobby also foresaw the rise of the "religious right" that would transpire during the next decade.

> *History seems often to glide in a smooth current for a time, until certain forces, gathering like a brewing storm, break forth to ruffle the surface and alter the direction of flow.* (Cross, 113)

> *Thus ultraists could justify proposing a Christian party in politics, and take upon themselves as converted men full responsibility for dictating to lesser fellow beings, in a fashion which to skeptical folk might seem the very perversion of democracy.* (Cross, 207)

> *There is nothing to which the minds of good men, when once passed the bounds of sound discretion, and launched on the ocean of feeling and experiment, may not come ... nothing so terrible and unmanageable as the fire and whirlwind of human passion, when once kindled by misguided zeal.... For, in every church, there is wood, hay, and stubble which will be sure to take fire on the wrong side.* (Lyman Beecher, quoted in Cross, 210)

DP: *I cannot be yours
   so you will seek another.
He will be the other season from me,
   will be summer, will be late warm afternoons,
   dry air, dry leaves, dry hair.
He will drop the sun before you like an apple.
You will pause, will be his, will be there.*

NOB: Is that yours?

DP: Yes, part of "Atalanta." I wrote it for LK, when our ménage was breaking up.

NOB: I've been reading about Mormonism, you know that.

DP: Yes, *The Refiner's Fire*.[59]

NOB: I think that the last religious upwelling in America was the 1840s, and that Mormonism is the American religion. I've got a lead on some Mormon theological works.[60]

DP: Oh dear.

NOB: (Silence)

DP: I mean, that sounds interesting.

NOB: That's better.

DP: I invited the Mormon missionaries in when I was a teen to talk theology with them. They believe that God has the form of a man and can only be at one place at a time.

NOB: (Signs of consternation) I don't understand the framework yet, so when I hear these off-the-wall facts, like that one, I can't see how they connect.

(I didn't have an answer, and after a few steps Nobby continued.)

NOB: Are there any Methodist theologians?

DP: I don't think so.

61 *"The complacent husband is a secure and willful Actaeon."* (A/M 36)

Hence, wearing the horns, the cuckold's horns, and being horn-mad.

Nobby thought there was something wrong with his "Actaeon," but it may be his best piece of poetry, even better than (the perhaps more finely crafted) "Daphne." And consider, he wrote through the heart of Robert Graves' territory, composing a hymn to goddess worship, without once mentioning (or needing to mention) the "white goddess."

62 I had given Nobby a copy of the galleys earlier, and Nobby had given me a critique—if it can be called that. Nobby had led me into his study at his home, through the kitchen and down a couple of stairs. "Come back to my torture chamber," he had said. That should have alerted me. It didn't.

Nobby's desk was in the center of the room, favoring the inside wall, and Nobby sat behind it. Like most of the rooms in my own house, the walls were lined with books. Nobby motioned for me to sit in the chair opposite the desk and folded his hands. For the next hour he demolished the book, its author, and its intent. From time to time I tried to respond with some lame defense, but mostly I just listened, too stunned to even take notes. Besides, what defense is there to "not serious philosophy," "why did you even write this?", "who could it possibly be for?", and "it will be identified as a drug book and no one will take it seriously." He left no stone on top of any other. Toward the end of the long harangue, as criticisms such as "it avoids the big questions, like Freud or Jung" started cropping up, I began to take heart, at least a little, but mostly I was dazed. When he finally ended I was able to mutter a choked "thank you" as I got up to go. As Nobby saw me to the door he said, "It did get me to thinking about intoxication, I admit that." And as I left he added, "Oh, by the way, the jab against science was okay."

I drove out to the cliffs above the ocean and parked and wrote down everything I could remember of what Nobby had said. In a funny way I felt empowered: what now had I to fear from critics?

I have since learned that Brown was notorious for the brutality of his attacks on his graduate students, and on his friends in >>

NOB: I can't think of any either.

DP: I think the Mormons lost their moral standing when they gave up polygamy.

NOB: I can see why you would think so.

DP: Your *ad hominem* attacks will get you nowhere.

(That brought a smile and Nobby picked up the pace.)

DP: Is "seeing the goddess naked" being cuckolded? You once told me that I would "never see the goddess naked."[61]

(I was hoping to get another revelation here, but Nobby changed the subject. I was surprised that he didn't take the bait, his usual voyeuristic mode would have been to query my last sentence.)

NOB: I've looked more carefully at your *Pharmako/Poeia*.[62]

DP: Ah. So now you know the extent of my perfidy.

NOB: Now I see how you've stolen all of my best ideas!

DP: (Smiles, walks ...)

NOB: In *Pharmako/Poeia*, you present poetry as literal truth, there is not enough playfulness.

DP: (Exasperated) But, in the ether chapter I talk about the *"ba-ba"* and *"ba-ba ba-ba-ba."* I give it a whole paragraph!

NOB: Hmm, well, I'll look again.

>> general. Several of his students were reduced to tears, and some never recovered. One, delivering his dissertation by hand, was dismissed with "I don't have time for that." He had only one female Ph.D. It wasn't until Nobby's memorial that I learned from another professor that Nobby actually liked *Pharmako/Poeia*.

63 *Beyond the reality-principle is poetry
taking metaphors seriously
(metaphors and analogics)
That way madness lies.*
(NOB, Harvard, March 20, 1967)

(This was about as much praise as I could ever get. We walked and Nobby continued.)

NOB: The problem is that there is no separation between the science and the non-science. You can't tell when it is science or a flight of fantasy.

DP: Surely YOU are not saying that there should be a wall between the science and the "non-sense."

NOB: In that case you need an epistemological preface, to explain what you are doing.

DP: If someone needs that wall, I'm not sure I have anything to say to them. I'm not writing for everyone.

NOB: Not for everyone? No, I part with you there.

(I was thinking about that. We kept walking.)

NOB: How would you feel when you were doing this mixing?

DP: I felt a powerful sense of transgression; that I was sinning.

NOB: Good!

DP: I enjoyed it immensely.

NOB: The problem is that you present poetry as literal truth. If what you are saying is poetry, I don't disagree with you; I have no problem. But you are speaking it as literal truth.

DP: The experiment is to willingly suspend the distinction—that science is metaphorical also—and then see what happens.

NOB: (Very bothered) Where did you get this speaking poetry as literal truth?

DP: From you![63]

NOB: But "all is poetry" is archaic, it's out of fashion. What do we mean when we say "all is poetry"? That is the question and you have to answer it yourself.

(Desultory walking followed. The trail emerged from the forest and we were in full sunlight again.)

NOB: I think you put in too much meaning, and not enough nothing.

(This one was deadly. I had no answer. Nobby smelled blood and pressed his attack.)

NOB: So why is it, do you think, that I don't just gobble up your phrases? What do you think the problem with me is?

DP: (Annoyed) You haven't destroyed enough of your brain with drugs.

NOB: So, you are just for those druggies!

DP: (Smiling) No, no. There are some in whom it is congenital.

NOB: You need drugs to overcome your Oedipus complex.

(We climbed over a fence. I was angry now and tired of this Oedipus stuff. I tried a counterattack.)

DP: Your problem is with chance.

NOB: (Laughs)

DP: Intellectual understanding of chance is not enough. That is the path of the Pharisees. Verily I say unto you, you must also gamble.

(Nobby was smiling, his chin slightly raised, but I wasn't finished.)

DP: I think you have some kind of a religious taboo against entering the sanctuary of chance—something to do with your mother's bedroom.

[64] *J. J. Bachofen:* **Motherright:** *An Analytic Summary prepared by Norman O. Brown with the Assistance of Sanford L. Segal.*

[65] I was thinking of Eve as a *curandera*—praising and tending the sacred tree.

[66] Justice as "severe poetry."

> *That the Ancient Roman Law Was a Serious Poem, and the Ancient Jurisprudence a Severe Kind of Poetry.* (Vico, *New Science,* 1027)

(I watched his face. I had been expecting a spirited retort, but Nobby just sighed and nodded his head gravely.)

NOB: I wrote a hundred-page essay on Bachofen, *Motheright*. Bachofen influenced Engels and Marx.[64]

DP: I want a copy. Did Freud read him?

NOB: I'm not sure. See George Thomson on Bachofen, he tried to bring him up to date, *Aeschylus and Athens*, and *Ancient Greek Society*. Bachofen is good on Orestes.

(We had passed the lime kiln again, and had reached the point where the trail led up along the river to the crossing.)

NOB: Freud was approaching the mother in the twenties, but I think Nazism scared him back to *Totem & Taboo*. And justice.

DP: Without the power of the mothers it's all warped, it's all dictatorial fathers. Then Hobbes claims that that is the state of nature.

NOB: Blake is relevant here.

DP: Yes, and Milton.[65]

(The trail was single file here, and brushy. Nobby walked on ahead for awhile, then half-turned to ask his next question.)

NOB: Why is *Paradise Lost* a failure?

DP: That admitting Evil is the same as admitting Justice?[66]

(Nobby's statement had taken me by surprise: I hadn't known that Paradise Lost *was a failure.... I was thinking about Blake's observation that Milton "wrote in fetters when writing of the angels" and "was of the Devil's party without knowing it.")*

NOB: Do you know Christopher Hill's Milton book, *Milton and the English Revolution*?

DP: No, but I bought his book on *The English Bible*.

67 *1 Henry IV*, ii, 3.

NOB: What does that say?

DP: That having the Bible led to discussions of interpretation, and that if the Bible could be interpreted, so could the King. The Catholics did not think that the demos should have the Bible.

NOB: Right. The Church was an oligarchy.

(We reached the river crossing and that interrupted the conversation, but Nobby picked it up as we were climbing up the opposite canyon to the road and the parking area.)

NOB: The question of esoteric knowledge also relates to the drug question.

DP: I'm very glad that now, at the end of our walk, you have completed the circle. Yes, it relates to the drug question very much. Aldous Huxley thought that psychedelics were inappropriate for commoners.

NOB: "Out of this nettle danger, we pluck this flower safety."[67]

(We were back at the car. I noticed that it was long after five, Nobby's curfew hour, but he didn't seem fazed. My legs were sore and tired and I was glad to be driving again.)

DP: Giving entheogenic drugs to the masses is like printing the Bible in English.

NOB: Don't use that.

DP: Why not?

NOB: There is a flaw in it somewhere.

DP: A flaw? A flow? A fly in the smooth smotherly anointment? Surely we do not wait to be sure there is no flaw before we present a thesis?

NOB: No, I've gotten beyond that one.

(When we got back to Nobby's driveway, we went over our book exchanges. Nobby wanted to read something on evolutionary biology, and wanted my opinion on whether he should read Weiner or Ridley. I liked Weiner, hadn't read The Beak of the Finch, *but said that I would give him a copy of a review I had of Dennett's book,* Darwin's Dangerous Idea. *He also wanted to borrow Evans,* The God of Ecstasy. *I said that I would include a book called* On Killing, *by Lt. Col. Dave Grossman. Nobby was to give me a copy of his manuscript on Bachofen.)*

NOB: Were there any other books that I was supposed to give you?

DP: I want a hardback of *Hermes the Thief*, signed. And you promised to will me your Joyce concordance.

(Nobby had a tendency to get a little morbid about death at times. I took every opportunity to needle him.)

NOB: Oh yes, when I am dead.

DP: Bye.

NOB: Good walk, see you.

DP: Oh, by the way, I heard a story that at one of your readings of *Apocalypse and/or Metamorphosis*, two young women in the front row undressed themselves. Did that really happen?

NOB: (Big smile. Touched his hat with his cane) Bye bye.

[1] Busted! I was writing my cocaine chapter for *Pharmako/Dynamis*, and doing fieldwork. I didn't think it showed.

SUNSET BEACH, JANUARY 1996

(Nobby had checked the tide chart and suggested that we go to Sunset Beach. A low tide was necessary to be able to walk around some of the headlands and bluffs.

We weren't even in the car when Nobby looked me in the eyes and asked me his first question.)

NOB: Are you taking some kind of stimulant, or narcotics?[1]

DP: Why do you ask?

NOB: Your eyes have an extra brightness. You are usually depressed, or in that mode.

DP: Interesting observation.

NOB: I think that my fear of drugs is more than just American Puritanism.

DP: What, say more.

2 *Freud considered this word to be one of the triumphs of the German language, as it has a flexibility that the standard English translation "instinct" does not. The German word* Instinkt, *which Freud uses only rarely, has the same connotations as the English instinct in the sense of "innate" and "inherited" biological structures.* Trieb, *however, is defined by Freud as "bodily inasmuch as they represent an incentive to mental activity." it is the crossover from mere bodily or reflexive hungers to the mental, or the reflective—the creative—that is crucial in Freud's use of the term....* (David Greenham, *The Resurrection of the Body,* 50)

3 "This was to be the climax of his contribution: the underlying fear to be dealt with/got through/transmogrified is the fear of chance/change/risk—very much as in Buddhism and in pharmakognostic practice—exposed in the form of the gods." (Tom Marshall, personal communication)

4 Coyote = Dionysus, as a foil to Divine Justice, was well enough established to pass without comment.

5 Displays so excessive that they are life-threatening, maladaptive. So love is an artist.

NOB: It is a fear, because of my pharmocophilia, with alcohol. I connect it with death, the death instinct.

DP: I'm uncomfortable with "instinct."

NOB: I am also. How about drive? The German word is *Trieb. Tod Trieb.*[2]

DP: Okay.

NOB: You have to look at death and evolution. I'm trying to replace the Freudian death instinct with some idea of chance. Risk. And you have to look at species versus the individual.[3]

(We talked of personal matters as we drove down the coast. Nobby knew where to park and how to get in. It was a lovely day: a few high clouds and a light breeze. We both wore jackets.)

We walked out over the beach to the hard sand. I pointed out some of the dune plants: Erysimum ammophilum, *a rare endemic wallflower, and some others. Sandpipers, piles of stranded kelp, the sound of the surf, the waves moving up and back on the beach, and the blue of the ocean gave us our backdrop.)*

NOB: What is your theory of death?

DP: (Walks a while before answering) Coyote brought death into the world, that's what I heard.[4]

NOB: Can you say that another way?

DP: The deer is a knife. That is, the doe's eye trims the deer, like the current of a stream trims the trout. So death is an artist.

NOB: You have to relate that to chance and risk.

DP: Maybe the antlers, exuberance. Wonderful sexual displays.[5]

(Nobby let that pass and we walked on for awhile. Sometimes a wave would make us skip up higher onto the beach to get out of the way.)

[6] Michel Serres, *The Parasite*: the three actors are host, guest, and the interrupter. The interrupter is noise, or parasite. Of course, in Serres' dialectic, the guest is also a parasite.

[7] The dialectic is too linear, so it needs "radical disruption" to obliterate, to disrupt the question, so it becomes a farce (or force).

[8] Nietzsche: "That which does not kill us makes us stronger." The *pharmakon* is both poison and remedy.

[9] Guest and host are both from PIE **ghos-ti* (Pokorny, 453). Lynn Margulis suggests that all symbiosis begins with parasitism. Vaccination is homeopathy, treating like with like. The "poison path," as outlined in *Pharmako/Poeia*, is seeking the cure from within the disease.

[10] *What does that synthesis of god and goat in the satyr mean? (Nietzsche). I estimate the value of human beings, or races, according to how necessarily they cannot understand the god apart from the satyr.*

Said the joker to the priest. (CT 60)

NOB: How do you see drugs in Serres's system?[6]

DP: The uninvited guest.

NOB: In the *Symposium*, Alcibiades barges in and raises the discourse to a whole new level.[7]

DP: So the parasite is the *pharmakon*, the poison that interrupts, and thus can strengthen.[8]

NOB: In vaccination, poison can be a cure. Serres. But you have to look at the whole context: parasitology, the host, hostility, hospitality.[9]

DP: The death drive seems to have more to do with Darwin than a drive, as such.

NOB: With generations, families, you have to deal with death.

DP: But it takes love *and* death to hold things together, doesn't it?

NOB: That's what they say. What is death alone?

DP: Ideology.

NOB: Touché. Good.

DP: (Thinking)

NOB: The *Symposium* is Plato's only farce, philosophy's only farce. You need farce to escape Dante and eschatology.[10]

(The surf seemed to be building. We moved up to the dry sand and walked through the ice plant and the other dune plants: beach primrose, sea rocket, and dune grass. Nobby brought up Pound, I suppose as antipodal to farce, and mentioned a book that had been dedicated to him by a former UCSC student that separated out Pound's fascism from his avant-garde. Nobby mentioned that the first Canto bore out that thesis. Somehow we got to Swinburne.)

[11] Cocaine, like all the stimulants, seems to narrow the focus, to lose the periphery. Poetic flights of reverie have a tendency to become literal. I investigate this in more detail in *Pharmako/Dynamis*.

NOB: Swinburne says no God, no Creator, no Savior:

> For whom all winds are quiet as the sun,
> All waters as the shore.

(We walked on. As if to cap his words, we passed a dead bird washed up on the sand. Nobby opened a new thread.)

NOB: What are you reading?

DP: Freud.

NOB: Good! About time ... What part?

DP: Cocaine. There may be a connection between psychoanalytic theory and cocaine. Experiencing a different state of consciousness under cocaine implied that there *were* other states of consciousness, that there isn't just one kind of consciousness.

NOB: Fair. You're still okay.

(We talked more about Freud and cocaine. Nobby wanted details, dates.)

DP: There is no evidence for cocaine use in later Freud ... Well, except for *Totem and Taboo*.

NOB: How do you mean?

DP: The story about the primal family: that seems to me to be de facto evidence of cocaine use.[11]

(Nobby let that pass. I had given Nobby William James's paper on nitrous oxide, and the talk turned to James.)

DP: A man named Beddoes opened a "Pneumatic Institute." Coleridge and Southey both went there, and Humphrey Davy.

NOB: (Unimpressed) James has a prosy style.

DP: Kind of pedestrian, you mean?

NOB: Yes. James never flew for me.

DP: He has a common sense that is refreshing.

[12] Blake, "Proverbs of Hell." Cf. Nietzsche: "What serves the higher type of men as nourishment or delectation must almost be poison for a very different and inferior type." (*Beyond Good and Evil*, 30)

[13] "Have you understood me?"

[14] Such as his never-ending multiplication of characters and complexity.

[15] As long as we're talking about the canon ...

NOB: Common sense never interested me. That was Freud's problem. That's the problem with psychoanalysis. They tried to make it common sense.

(More walking.)

NOB: James's father was a Swedenborgian. Swedenborg is Blake. How do you feel about Blake?

DP: Kind of between God and the archangel Gabriel.

NOB: (Petulantly) God! You still believe in God. You can't walk with me!

DP: "One law for the lion and the ox is oppression."[12]

NOB: Yes. But I worked that all out with Marx.

(We walked some more. I was wondering what that meant.)

NOB: Marxist determinism will not do. Freudian determinism will not do.[13]

(More walking, to let the point settle.)

DP: Every so often I come to a problem with Blake and think I'll have to let him go, but he always manages to come back.[14]

NOB: He's a giant.

DP: I was shocked that he wasn't included in the "canon" in my daughter's class on the Romantics.

NOB: Neither the *London Times Literary Supplement* nor the *NY Review of Books* ever mentions NOB.[15]

DP: Camille Paglia addresses the subject of the canon.

NOB: I read *Sexual Personae*. I liked it, but I don't think it will have much impact on the "canon."

(We were in a flat area, and had to retreat up the beach before a wave.)

16 That sobriety is not the opposite of inebriation; nor is sobriety our "normal" state.

17 *Dionysus has returned to his native Thebes; mind—at the end of its tether—is another Pentheus up a tree. Resisting madness can be the maddest way of being mad.... It is possible to be mad and to be unblest; but it is not possible to get the blessing without the madness; it is not possible to get the illumination without the derangement.* ("Apocalypse," A/M, 2)

18 Gk *stasis*, a standing, standing still; *existanai*, to put (*histanai*) out of (*ex-*) place, to derange, so *ekstasis*, Late Latin *ecstasis*, a trance, standing out.

19 Meanwhile, Coyote breaks the rules, colors outside the lines, goes out of his mind, AND loses his way.

NOB: Paglia is secular. It has to be religious, I think. It has to be religious to succeed. Secular attempts will fail. Marxism failed.

DP: If it has to be religious, then it will lose to orthodoxy three out of four seasons.

(Uncontested. More walking. The conversation returned to intoxication.)

DP: Perhaps the problem is with sobriety, and *ebriety* informs that.[16]

NOB: Yes. You have to look at madness. See NOB, Phi Beta Kappa.[17]

DP: Madness is mead. Do you know anything about mead as the food of the gods?

NOB: *Trimma* was the wine drunk at the theater. There were women brewers. And you have to look at the girls at *pannychis*, a women's festival in midwinter. Aristophanes. And Dodds, *ygra phusis*.

DP: (After taking notes) Can you tell me anything about *sobria ebrietas*? I think it's in Philo.

NOB: Philo the Jew! Yes. There was some writing about *sobria ebrietas* in German. It's old and may be hard to find. There may even have been a journal.

DP: A Spanish philosopher, Antonio Escohotado, sets up ecstatic, visionary inebriation against drunken loss of control, or delirium, where you don't remember anything.

NOB: Delirium is out of line, down from the furrow. Ecstasy is standing out.[18]

DP: So ecstasy is derangement, but not losing one's way?[19]

NOB: How do you see that?

DP: The interrupted meal.

20 *Dais*, meal; *daisis*, division of property; from the cutting up of the sacrifice. Latin *dominium* is also a feast or banquet. Hermes interrupts Baucis and Philemon. The stranger entering the city is Dionysus—Θεοδαίσιος, "Theodaisios" is one of his epithets. Prometheus, like Coyote and Raven, is the interrupter. *Akletos daitaleus*, the uninvited banqueter, refers to the eagle who eats Prometheus's liver. Thus we have fire.

Brown noted that Marxism picks up from Shelly: Prometheus, revolt, overthrowing the powers that be. However, Prometheus was responsible for installing Zeus in the first place. "Humanism thinks there is a technical solution, but technique does not have a solution to the problem of technology. Prometheanism will not save us." (NOB, from a lecture)

In Hesiod, Zeus's victory is aided by an armament industry (Cyclopes), and a mercenary army (the Hundred-Arms). After the victory Zeus builds prisons. Like Cortez, Zeus used cunning (μῆτις) and "statesmanship." Zeus swallowed Metis, his first wife, so that Athena would be born from his own head, allowing him to harness and channel the violence of his children, and thus avoid the fate of the failed hegemony of Sky and Kronos (as also in the myth of Tiamat and Marduk).

21 Jacques Derrida has a playful essay on this subject: "Plato's Pharmacy."

NOB: Yes. The feast of the gods, as in Homer. The dinner was getting ugly, there was fighting over the sacrifice. Prometheus helped man. *Theodaisia*: division, dominance. *Theoxenia* is hospitality, because that's what you give to strangers.[20]

DP: The uninvited guest of course is Dionysus.

NOB: But you are trying to say that anyone who revels, that it all comes from drugs. But there is a difference between us, you take drugs and I don't.

(Nobby got very moralistic, and, I thought, pedestrian. But I stumbled along in the farce.)

DP: Sure you take drugs.

NOB: No.

DP: Do you drink coffee?

NOB: No.

DP: But I say that reading is a drug. And writing is certainly a drug, and I can claim Socrates as company on that.

NOB: What?

DP: *Phaedrus,* Socrates calls writing a *pharmakon.*[21]

NOB: What isn't a *pharmakon*?

DP: (Mistakenly starts thinking, and lays a bomb) Basic sanity?

NOB: Uggh! You can't go for walks with me talking about things like basic sanity. Uggh. Your father has triumphed!

DP: (Shamed, tries to save something from it all) Okay, maybe all things are *pharmakon*. Certainly sensation is a drug experience.

NOB: How?

22 NOB recognized history as a reflection of the war among the gods, *theomachy*. Plants and plant poisons are the warriors and angels of the gods. Some plants take over whole continents. And they have their own politics: alcohol and opium don't get along; there are frequent scraps between alcohol and hashish. Alcohol, while belligerent, seems to have forged an alliance with tobacco. Tobacco seems to get along with everyone, which is why it is the great diplomat. (Pendell, *Pharmako/Poeia: Plant Powers, Poisons, and Herbcraft*)

23 "The Gray Lovers," on sharing love (see final Appendix, p.225). Nobby's son, Tom Brown, told me that Nobby had it taped to his bathroom mirror when he died, along with Shelly's "Ode to the West Wind."

24 In *The Parasite*, the country rat tries to escape risk and interruptions. He goes back to the country, denying the chancy world for the utopia of geometry, justice, and "security." But as Serres points out, that requires constant wakefulness. If sleep enters, if the darkness enters, if there are any shadows or unseen corners, the parasite re-enters. Constant wakefulness equals grammar equals repression equals oppression equals the police state. The city rat gets used to interruptions, accepts the risk as part of his life and lives with it.

What is this in terms of Freudian repression? (I wish I had asked Nobby.) Repression is denial, the country rat going home, unable to face the complexity, the noise, the injustice of it all. Unable to face one's own shadow, in Jungian terms. In Freud, it must be the primal scene that is being repressed, the murder of the father. Guilt interrupts the meal. For the country rat, the city, along with all of its guilty horrors, is banished from consciousness.

As, for example, in drug laws: we want no excess, no abuse, no reminder of greed, lust, or weakness. We banish masturbation. We torture and kill the addicts and settle into our comfortable neuroses, medicated by corporate drugs. Just knowing about the city rat disturbs us: the city rat is, after all, a parasite. Denying the Stranger at the door is hostility: the ego denying the id, the superego denying the ego. (Cf. Serres, *The Parasite*, part 2)

DP: Well, electromagnetic waves come through the eyes, they stimulate chemical reactions, which cause other chemical reactions, finally there is a bunch of rhodopsin, melatonin, serotonin, things like that, and we have a hallucination of vision.

NOB: I'd hate to have to face you in a debate.

DP: You did say you had an affair with alcohol.

NOB: (Began to say that alcohol was not a drug, but stopped himself) Why is it that we don't consider alcohol a drug? And why is alcohol okay and not the others?

(Now Nobby was in my territory.)

DP: It has to do with the diplomacy and psychology of the War of Poisons. Alcohol is jealous, selfish. Maybe also insecure. Maybe that's because of its anality.[22]

NOB: How's that?

DP: Alcohol is excrement, from yeast.

(Nobby let that stand for ten yards, then tried an attack on the flank.)

NOB: Your poem, on Baucis and Philemon, is not very Dionysian.[23]

(Just, I suppose, to even the score. Nobby liked the poem and I didn't argue his point. We continued along the beach, trying to find the strip of hard sand between the water and the soft dunes.)

NOB: Baucis and Philemon are in Serres. And you should look at *Faust, Part Two*.

(Nobby's reading suggestions kept me busy. I had my own thoughts on Serres.)[24]

NOB: Serres is a scientist. This should be familiar territory for you. What is Maxwell's Demon?

January 1996   157

[25] Recent discoveries have found that Maxwell's Demon can enter by chance, that pockets of order occur spontaneously within a thermodynamic system at equilibrium. Perpetual motion, banished from the *Republic*, knocks again at the city gate. All that is needed is a diode, a revolving nano-door on a ratchet. Hope springs eternal. Richard Feynman critiques the ratchet-demon in a general way in his *Lectures on Physics*, Chapter 46.

[26] As in Pascal: chance leads to statistics, statistics to the group, where n = 1 has minimal significance. Nobby related that to *The Disappearance of God*, by J. Hillis Miller, which he was reading. Marshall points out that for Brown, the individual was "relatively nonexistent—what exists is the species taking on forms—all questions must be addressed to it [the species]." (Tom Marshall, personal communication)

(Nobby let me be the informant for awhile, and I accepted gratefully. I told him about Maxwell's Demon, explaining as best I could. Maxwell's Demon opens and closes a tiny door between two fluids or gases at the same temperature, letting the faster, more energetic molecules through one way, and the slower, cooler molecules the other way, thus creating a thermal gradient. Serres put Maxwell's Demon at the throat, as the constriction of the hourglass, and then made the hourglass an image of the parasite, dividing.)

DP: Maxwell's Demon is a challenge to the Second Law of Thermodynamics, to chance.[25]

(The Second Law states that entropy only moves one direction, and that the Demon must expend more energy than is stored in the gradient.

Nobby, rather astutely, wanted to know when the mass overtook the individual, and when time became irreversible, but before I could formulate a response, threading from Maxwell to Feynman, Nobby moved ahead.)

NOB: God, or Dionysus, cannot affect the individual, only masses.[26]

(More discussion followed on the attempts to explain ("explain away") altruism. We want to be told that egoism is our true nature, all the while suspecting that acquisitiveness is sin. We want to be assured that "self interest" is the true religion, without knowing what the "self" is.)

NOB: You have to lay a wager.

DP: Pascal's wager was pretty lame, not like Kierkegaard.

NOB: I never took to Kierkegaard. How was Pascal lame?

DP: Well, he worked out all the odds by figuring. The odds were overwhelmingly in favor of one, so he chose it. All common sense—that sometimes it is rational to gamble.

NOB: And Kierkegaard?

[27] Daniel C. Dennett, *Darwin's Dangerous Idea*. Dennett tries to root out any trace of vitalism, magical thinking, or teleology in evolutionary thought, referring to such attempts as "sky hooks."

[28] Francis Crick, the co-discoverer of the structure of DNA, denies all meaning to dreams (mental garbage), and even locates a "Seat of the Soul," the residence of free will, in the anterior cingulate sulcus. Interestingly, Crick had experience with LSD, thus proving once again that LSD does not automatically endow one with mystical consciousness.

[29] None of the "hard AI" crowd have yet refuted Roger Penrose's proof (in *Shadows of the Mind*) that consciousness is non-computational.

DP: A cliff.

NOB: Yes. He ended up in Christianity though.

DP: So did Pascal, you're not holding that against them, are you?

NOB: (Smiling) I was about to make an allowance for Pascal.

DP: Ah, but by Kierkegaard's time he should have known better!

NOB: Yes!

DP: Doesn't the wager have telos written all over it?

NOB: So you will wager the same as your father, and I wager the same as my mother.

(A typical NOB conversation stopper. We scrambled around some cliffs. A group of four pelicans flew by, skimming over the water. The ground was littered with fallen branches.)

NOB: Look at all those wagers.

(We walked further. Both of us had been reading Dennett.)

NOB: Dennett won't do.[27]

DP: I don't trust the smugness.

NOB: I wish I could wipe the grin off of their faces. Maybe Dionysus will make them laugh.

DP: I think Crick is a worthier opponent.[28]

NOB: Dennett's "sky hook" is too rhetorical. There's a chauvinism there.

DP: There's a dualism, intellect apart from nature. In spite of their attempt to reduce consciousness to an "epiphenomenon" of computation.[29]

30 Wendy Brown, *States of Injury, Power and Freedom in Late Modernity*. Judith Butler, *Gender Trouble, Feminism and the Subversion of Identity*. Nobby said that Wendy Brown's philosophical style was "not his way." Nonetheless he spent several months writing Wendy Brown a fourteen page letter.

31 *The attacks on nature and wilderness from the ivory towers come at just the right time to bolster developers, the resurgent timber companies and those who would trash the Endangered Species Act. It looks like an unholy alliance of Capitalist Materialist and Marxist Idealists in an attack on the rural world that Marx reputedly found idiotic and boring.* (Gary Snyder, "Is Nature Real," in *The Gary Snyder Reader*)

32 In "The Turn to Spinoza," "God = Nature" DOES "do," if the political side of the monism isn't ignored:

> *Liberal individualists (Stuart Hampshire) interpret the monism, reduced to the aphoristic equation God = Nature, as a moment of mystic feeling, a philosophic or rather quasi-religious posture of "identification with the whole of Nature," a purely mental act in the mind of the isolated and purely contemplative philosopher. It is not difficult to see a contradiction between Spinoza's monism, so interpreted, and his materialism. And even if there were no contradiction, Spinoza's monism would then have no more hold on us than Einstein's or Oppenheimer's private mystical or "oceanic" feelings....*
>
> *Spinoza's monism has been interpreted mystically. But if we interpret it politically, it can be seen as setting the historical agenda for us today: to rectify the flaw in modernity; to arrive at one world; to reorganize the gigantic material processes of intercommunication released by modernity into a coherent unity; call it Love's Body.* (A/M 128)

Brown puts Spinoza in line with Blake, that there is no soul apart from the body. Further, Brown approaches Mahayana Buddhist concepts, positing that through Spinoza (and Whitehead) the separate, independent self is an illusion. Against Hobbes (and Augustine), Brown states: "What is common is not simply the foundation of our reasoning, as common notions; communism »

NOB: I like Wendy Brown's attack on nature, that there is no natural sexuality. Reading the lesbians ... something in *Gender Trouble* reminds me that once in NOB polymorphous perversity was important.[30]

DP: No natural sexuality doesn't mean there is no nature.

NOB: You've given no arguments yet.

DP: Paul Shepard calls deconstructionism the intellectual wing of the theme park movement.

NOB: Say more, I can see that this is problematical for you. It is for me also.

DP: It is easy enough to critique nature as a concept, but then the post-modernists say that there is no reason to protect nature, that deep ecologists are just perpetuating phallocentric patriarchy.[31]

NOB: Spinoza's God = Nature won't do.[32]

DP: Anti-nature is in alliance with the Christian right. Maybe Jeffers can help.

NOB: How?

>> is good for us, or it is the good: 'Nothing can be evil through what it has in common with our nature.'" (*A/M* 131)

Lastly, in Spinoza, Brown finds an anarchistic political model:

> *This original approach to mass psychology developed in Spinoza's* Ethics *does not, as even Freud's does, envisage dependence on a leader, or head, as the origin or essence of mass formation.* (*A/M* 134)

33 Sessions' ideas are based on Arne Naess, *Freedom, Emotion, and Self-Subsistence: The Structure of a Central Part of Spinoza's Ethics*, University of Oslo, 1975, and essays by Naess and Paul Wienpahl in Jon Wetlesen, *Spinoza's Philosophy of Man*, Oslo, 1978.

34 Sontag points out that Brown thought that both Ferenczi (NOB called him "the favored disciple") and Reich erred in accepting the "primacy of the orgasm," but that this was less important than that they understood the political implications of Freud's ideas:

> *They are far truer to Freud than the orthodox psychoanalysts who, as a result of their inability to transform psychoanalysis into social criticism, send human desire back into repression again.* (Sontag, *Against Interpretation*)

At another time Nobby said that homosexuals liked *LAD* because it was genital.

35 *Conium maculatum*: κωνειον. Pliny mentions that this "traditional punishment" also has salutary effects. As Paracelsus said, it is all in the dose.

36 Keats, "Ode to a Nightingale."

DP: George Sessions connected Spinoza and Jeffers through pantheism, "Be born of the rock, not a woman."[33]

(Nobby didn't respond. I tried again, and did better.)

DP: Jeffers also said, "I would rather, but for the penalties, kill a man than a hawk."

NOB: You have not been wasting your time by studying Jeffers.

(I was pleased with that and emboldened to open a new thread.)

DP: So where is it in *Life Against Death* that you talk about *coitus reservatus?*

NOB: It's between the lines, part of negating genital organization, the centralized state.[34]

(We crossed a little stream that came down to the beach. Hemlock was growing in profusion. We stopped.)

DP: This is hemlock. When Socrates said that he had nothing to learn outside of the city, he had to eat more than his words.

NOB: (Flustered) This plant? This is hemlock?

DP: The purple blotches are distinctive.

NOB: How do they know this is the same plant?

DP: *Conium.* We know from the old herbals, and from the description of the effects in *Phaedo.*[35]

NOB: My heart aches, and a drowsy numbness pains
    My sense, as though of hemlock I had drunk.[36]

(We walked on and picked up the thread on deconstructionism and the talk turned to Derrida. We were both in a very anti-Derrida mood that day. NOB called him a narcissist.)

DP: It's idealism, even solipsism. He loves his own cleverness and will obfuscate to indulge it.

[37] Mādhyamika is the school of Mahayana Buddhism founded by Nāgārjuna that "excludes all conceivable predicates to reality, whether they be of existence, of nonexistence, of neither existence nor nonexistence, or of both existence and nonexistence." (John Grimes, *A Concise Dictionary of Indian Philosophy*) Gayatri Spivak translated Derrida's *Of Grammatology*.

[38] Atheism leaves the problem of monotheism/polytheism unresolved, as did Brown. Atheism sidesteps the question, "*Which god is it you don't believe in?*" Even if one can't come up with any believable god, the exercise is worthwhile in itself. Similar questioning of believers usually reveals a great deal of difference as to just what the powers and characteristics of "God" are. "One God" can be viciously intolerant. As Nietzsche said, "The greatest advantage of polytheism is that choosing one god is not a blasphemy against the others." Monotheism was the dream of putting an end to the family squabbling, but only Spinoza seems to have pulled it off.

NOB: He was corrupted by the fawning in American universities.

DP: Is Derrida a nihilist?

NOB: Yes, so it leads to his friend ... who was a fascist ... the Belgian, from Yale.

DP: Why does everyone like him so much?

NOB: Because they are stupid.

DP: Gayatri Spivak said that mādhyamika was wholly negative, but that Derrida affirmed woman.[37]

NOB: What does that mean? Derrida seems wholly negative to me. And I'm trying to fight that. It's a matter of the "nonconformist conscience." The nonconformist has to be more Christian than the Christians. I've been talking to Christopher Hill about that.

(I didn't respond. We walked some more. Nobby told me that I should read Derrida's piece on chance, "Mes Chances." I wrote it down. Nobby said he would give it to me.)

NOB: Wendy Brown and Judith Butler see atheism as an easy solution to Christianity. But in her atheism the morality is conventional. She hasn't seen the Blakean union of opposites.

DP: Isn't atheism still needing God?[38]

NOB: Logos is phallic. Judith Butler suppresses her wit, and her style, but though the words are taken out there is an underlying Christianity. They use contingency to avoid identities. But they misuse contingency, they ignore the unconscious. Why is there no unconscious in the post-Derrida feminists, or in your generation in general?

(I had no answer, so just kept walking.)

[39] Hegel's "Bacchanalian revel, in which no member is not drunk." (*Phenomenology of Mind*)

[40] Somehow we got to "peripheralize," joyful linguistic cunning, the sexualization of language through style.

> *Speech resexualized: overcoming the consequences of the fall. The tongue was the first unruly member. Displacement is first from above downwards; the penis is a symbolic tongue, and the disturbances of ejaculation a kind of genital stuttering.* (LB 251)

(Penises everywhere, unlike orthodox psychoanalysis and the reality principle which warn against the resexualizing of speech.)

[41] To paraphrase NOB again: psychoanalysis, begun to eliminate magical thought, finds that dreams are what we are made of.

> *Civilized objectivity is non-participating consciousness, consciousness as separation, as dualism, distance, definition; as property and prison: consciousness ruled by negation, which is from the death instinct. Symbolical consciousness, the erotic sense of reality, is a return to the principle of ancient animistic science, mystical participation, but now for the first time freely; instead of religion, poetry.* (LB 254)

> *In the buginning is the woid, in the muddle is the sounddance.* (FW 378)

[42] The Buddhist doctrine of *anātman* asserts that there is no Self, or Soul. But what was the Buddha really talking about? Cf. Gurdjieff and Ouspensky, who said that although we are not born with souls, our purpose here is to *grow* a soul. I once heard a literalist-minded Zen teacher scoff at this idea with a snort, not understanding that his own literalism constituted belief in "The Soul."

[43] The twelve-fold cycle of becoming, depicted on the Wheel of Life. Lama Govinda states that conditioned or dependent origination is not a law of causality.

> *All phases of this Dependent Origination are phenomena of the same illusion, the illusion of egohood. By overcoming this* >>

DP: Logos may be phallic, but language remains a drunken revel.[39] Logos is Huxley's ice cube: frozen concepts—the great challenge of the intellectual path.

NOB: You have to go from Pound to Joyce.[40]

DP: So: poetry, madness, love versus syntax, reason, atheism.[41]

(Nobby liked that.)

NOB: Do you believe in a soul?

DP: No.[42]

NOB: Contingency means there is no separate soul.

DP: In Buddhism there is the theory of dependent origination.[43]

NOB: I don't like the individual salvation of Buddhism, and there is no excess! Of course, that was before I met the estimable Vimalakirti. But I think that Buddhism is so large that you could find about anything in it.

(A wave chased us up the beach. I didn't feel like pursuing the Buddhist thread, so I returned to Derrida.)

DP: Is Derrida a determinist?

NOB: He comes up to indeterminacy but backs off.

(It was getting cold. We zipped up our jackets.)

NOB: Today's radicals can talk to the unconverted, not like the Marxists, who only tried to manipulate the Unbelievers.

>> *illusion, we step beyond the circle in which we imprisoned ourselves, and we realize that no thing and no being can exist in itself or for itself, but that each form of life has the whole universe as its basis and that therefore the meaning of individual form can only be found in its relationship to the whole.* (Lama Anagarika Govinda, Foundations of Tibetan Mysticism, 247)

[44] "A Child Is Being Beaten," Freud's *Collected Papers, Vol. II.*

[45] Such credential-attacks came every two or three years, usually when I was out of money, or when I had just heard some Dr. So-and-so say something really stupid and still be taken seriously.

DP: (I thought I must have misunderstood him.) You think so? It seems like the deconstructionists only talk to themselves. I myself do not attempt to reach the unconverted—I am only interested in those who have already lost their souls.

NOB: How is your writing going?

DP: I've been fighting with my Critic. My superego keeps saying "you can't do that, you're not good enough."

NOB: You long for the soul.

DP: So I made myself a scourge.

NOB: You did WHAT?

DP: A scourge, a cat-o'-nine-tails. I made it with leather cords, tied to a handle of bay laurel, and I knotted the cords with beads and wicked pieces of twisted wire. It's quite horrific looking. So whenever I hear the inner voices starting to beat up on me, I take out the scourge and give myself a couple of whacks across my back. I mean, why not bring it to the surface, if you know what I mean. I've even thought I could offer weekend seminars and workshops: "Scourge Your Way to Freedom."

NOB: Have you read Freud's essay, "A Child Is Being Beaten"?

DP: No.

NOB: Promise me that you will read it. It's in his *Collected Papers*. You have those, don't you?

DP: Yes. Okay.[44]

(*Nobby seemed positively gleeful. We were nearing the end of the walk. The tide was coming in fast and we had to time our run around some rocks with the ebb of the waves.*)

DP: So I've been thinking of going back to graduate school, going for a Ph.D.[45]

NOB: I don't think you should do that.

(I asked him why not and argued his points, but I couldn't budge him. I brought up a mutual friend, Tom Marshall, who was my age and had entered the Ph.D. program.)

NOB: It's fine for Tom Marshall, but it's *not* fine for you.

(I ran out of arguments. We were back at the parking lot. Later that year I separated from my wife. A friend offered me a cabin in the mountains above Calistoga, several hours to the north. Nobby was pretty unhappy with this development. I told him about it at the end of a walk to Fall Creek, that July, when we were back in his driveway. Nobby just said "Well, GOODBYE then!" And got out of the car.)

LAST WALK, FALL CREEK, MARCH 1997

(Since we hadn't seen each other for many months, NOB wanted to get caught up on my personal life. He found it exasperating, as usual.)

NOB: When I married, I knew it was for life.

DP: Who says it's not? We just can't live together.

NOB: That doesn't make sense to someone of my generation.

DP: I know, my father can't fathom it either.

NOB: You tried to explain it to him?

DP: Yes.

NOB: (Sighing) No, no. But how do you understand the breakdown of marriage, people just marrying on whims and divorcing casually?

DP: Nobby, I was married over twenty years. There was nothing casual about any of it.

[1] I had separated from my wife and was living in a tiny cabin in the mountains near Calistoga.

[2] A new addition to my nefarious dossier of "tendency" sins, along with "Jungian," and "academic."

[3] Peter Redgrove, *The Black Goddess and the Unseen Real*. Redgrove explores several of our lesser known sensory abilities, and examines evidence that electromagnetic pollution is smothering some of our subtler psychic senses.

NOB: I don't mean you, I mean generally.

DP: The culture is decadent.

NOB: I think we are doomed.

DP: Not clear that it's all a mistake ...

(Out of the car now, at Fall Creek, walking.)

NOB: How are you getting on up there? Where is it you are? Do you have any routines?[1]

DP: I'm doing okay. The solitude is new. I get a little crazy at times.

NOB: You mean it brings out your homosexual tendencies?[2]

DP: Yes, Nobby, that MUST be why I'm here with you. Actually, that doesn't seem to be the way it's going. Every woman I've ever smiled at has come by for a visit.

NOB: How is your mother?

DP: A pile of worry.

(We walked twenty or thirty yards in silence, both of us evidently musing over mothers and Oedipus. I was wondering what my mother saw in my father. None of this was said out loud, but Nobby was right with me.)

NOB: I just don't think I could articulate anything about my parents' relationship.

DP: Read a book by a man named Peter Redgrove.

NOB: Never heard of him.

DP: He's a poet. Just listen. He called his book *The Black Goddess*.[3] He thinks that Oedipus gave the wrong answer, that it is patriarchy that supports that answer.

NOB: You mean you think it is a vagina?

4 I was wondering if women had specialized in circle magic, medicines and blessings to hold the group together, as opposed to male shamanism focused on solitary vision quest.

5 *The thought, poem, is a cell or seed; a germ of living thought: growing from nothing to ripeness. Instead of the dead wood of systems, the tree of life; ramifications; branched thoughts new-grown with pleasant pain.* (LB 190)

DP: (Smiling) A woman, yes, that's what he says.

NOB: No. I don't think there IS any answer. And I think we are doomed because we can't solve it. Doomed.

DP: See, what I'm glimpsing is that the women, or some of them, have some knowledge here, and have had, for a long time. Maybe forty thousand years.[4]

NOB: I don't like your last sentence. It implies veneration for the past.

DP: (Sarcastically) Oh right! It is only NOW that we are intelligent. It is only NOW that we really know and can think ...

NOB: (Walks on, doesn't contest the point) What are you writing?

DP: I sent you some.

NOB: You did? I don't remember.

DP: Not a good sign ... The main progression is through the fragments.

NOB: What are the fragments?

DP: The parts between the chapters. The fragments are what is missing from science.

NOB: That's good. I hope you will use some of my chapter "Fraction."[5]

DP: A lot of what I'm doing has to do with the Feminine. And with women.

(More walking. I was thinking of Goethe. Nobby seemed to read my mind.)

NOB: It comes into *Faust*: the Mothers. In Part One, I think. That is a territory I have never fathomed. And now I am too old, thank God.

DP: Come on, Nobby, that won't do. And there is the whole "love" thing.

March 1997   179

[6] The heart of the troubadours: the "Love Court" at Poitiers. Was Eleanor of Aquitaine a dominatrix? "True love" as an exercise in stoking the fires of unconsummated desire to the breaking point: first you may only admire me from afar, later we will become companions, and spend time in each other's presence. At some point I will let you see me naked. Much later, we will sleep together, but we won't have sex. Then I'll let you pleasure me but without penetration. Finally, finally, at some point, I will let you enter me, but you must not have an orgasm.

NOB: Love won't do, it's too Christian. Dionysus!

(We crossed a bridge over the creek and paused, briefly, looking at the water.)

DP: If Christ is love, then Dionysus is ... dancing.

NOB: (Stops, confession time) You are looking at a man who has never danced.

DP: Your dancing is in your books. But I've been thinking of the troubadours.

NOB: They had a good theory.

DP: Not only a theory. They also had a practice.[6]

NOB: Yes, I have always believed that to be true.

DP: Go on.

NOB: Briffault. Robert Briffault: *The Mothers*. Three vols. It's old. I mean, he was writing when Frazer was writing.

DP: Some books don't go bad.

NOB: Right. Anyway, that's what I read. He was influenced by Engels. I'm not sure just how *The Origin of the Family* comes through it. He was a real scholar, not an imitation scholar like I am.

DP: (Quiet, thinking of himself as an imitation)

NOB: You have to look at Nietzsche and women. And at Ariadne. You do know who Ariadne is?

DP: Yes, teacher, I do know who Ariadne is.

NOB: The Greeks didn't do much with Dionysus and Ariadne. You never see anything.

DP: I've seen a relief, quite beautiful, but it may be Roman.

[7] "Supposed" ... at least by Hesiod and Apollodorus. But Nobby always had an inside scoop.

Some say that Dionysus's mother was Demeter or Io (Diodorus Siculus), others that she was Lethe, forgetfulness. Robert Graves notes that Semele was worshipped at Athens during the *Lenaea*, the "Festival of Wild Women." Jane Harrison notes that Dionysus, as Sabazius, was a beer god before a wine god.

[8] "Christ or Dionysus, have you understood me?"

[9] Finally.

NOB: About all I know is a letter, from that irascible poet Ovid. A letter of Ariadne's. But the real story is Semele. It is all obfuscated by the supposed love affair between Semele and Zeus.[7]

(We passed a large pool where two men and a woman had taken their clothes off and were sitting in a shaft of sunlight that was finding its way through the trees. A child splashed in the water.

I was thinking of the union of the patriarch and the moon: history, Crete. Nobby read my mind again.)

NOB: There is an island near Crete where Ariadne is buried. I went there.

DP: Back up Nobby, how does this relate to Nietzsche and women?

NOB: Don't you remember his last words? And what he said just as he slipped into madness?

DP: I KNOW what his last words were. Go on.[8]

NOB: When Nietzsche went mad, he believed that he WAS Dionysus.

(More walking.)

DP: If Dionysus truly appears, I shudder for my children.

NOB: Yes! Your understanding is correct.[9]

(We walked on, talked of the beauty of the scenery, the feel of the air, Chinese paintings, some personal things, and the Trillium in blossom.)

DP: The brutal efflorescence of spring.

NOB: That's good. Write that one down.

(I did.)

NOB: What's the etymology of brute? I don't think its Latin.

[10] He'd just proclaimed the New Gospel and was very pleased with himself. Apart from the Augustinian problem with justice, "love" was a glyph for whatever Freudian and Marxist determinism may lurk in *Love's Body*. "Chance" is the desperate and messianic dream for a second Dionysian birth.

I tried my best to salvage love, as love being divine madness, but without much success. Nobby retreated enough to say that maybe what we needed was a new word, that "love" wouldn't do.

Recently (*Nature*, April 12, 2007), scientists have found that photonic energy in chlorophyll is not transferred randomly, but that the chlorophyll molecules are in a state of extended quantum coherence (they saw the interference patterns of the waves). This means that the electron is able to explore all of the possible paths without going through them: it's all one wave. We can go from "wave" to "wife," following Snyder (*Earth House Hold*, *Regarding Wave*) and Eric Partridge. From "wife" we get to "love" through one of the oldest poems in English, "Praise of Women," Robert Mannyng of Brunne. So I would now respond, "Not chance, love!" I await your answer, dear teacher.

[11] Unlike Fortuna, chance tends to be monotheistic. In Dennett, chance denies all "sky-hooks," which is really saying that there are no *other* sky-hooks but chance. Metaphor may get lip service, but only chance wears the grammar of Truth. My point is that chance (in the reductionist sense) = Single Vision, and is a denial of Blake's "Imagination." So what we're looking for is a polytheistic "chance."

[12] Our positions had reversed. Fourteen years earlier I had written:

> *Dear NOB,*
> *it won't work*
> *they will not return*

In 1971 Brown taught a class titled "To Greet the Return of the Gods," recording his lectures beforehand so that he could "participate" in the class instead of lecturing. The textbook was called *Book of Ours*, text by NOB, calligraphed and illustrated by Nor Hall. >>

DP: Not sure. Do you think that Dionysus was a philanderer?

NOB: No! He was far beyond that.

DP: But you don't think it is love.

NOB: Not love. Chance![10]

(There was so much we could leave unsaid at that point, so we just walked further, then stopped and sat on a log.)

DP: Blake is not so easily dismissed.[11]

NOB: No. I agree. Blake is not so easily dismissed. We're together there.

DP: But see, we can accept chance as messages from the gods.

NOB: I tried that. It doesn't work. There was a book I never wrote: *To Greet the Return of the Gods*. It's listed as one of my publications in *Closing Time*.[12]

>> As a book, *To Greet the Return of the Gods* was alive at least as late as 1973. "Daphne" and "Actaeon" were evidently the first two installments, but Nobby seems to have gotten stuck somewhere in "Narcissus": "But Narcissus ... there I drowned." Something frightened Brown away from poetry:

> *Or paralyzed by the proximity:* iste ego sum — *Could it be me? Narcissus is undone discovering his identity with his own reflection; we are undone discovering our identity with Narcissus.* ("Narcissus," *A/M*, 143)

Or maybe it was because he lost his muse (renounced her, actually) — that wild, free woman who could bring all the myths into a living present. "No man could defeat him," but he couldn't seem to get past Sor Juana. Or was it M. C.?

Curiously, there is no mention of Echo anywhere in Brown's "Narcissus" essay. Rather narcissistic!

DP: That you never wrote it means that it is the secret text between the lines of your other books.... That's just to show you that I wasn't sleeping in class, professor.

(Nobby smiled wryly.)

NOB: John Cage almost got there. He brought in chance. But I think that the confrontation with chance was too stark for his Christian background. He couldn't take the next step.

(We walked further. I pointed out some of the plants we passed: elk clover, coltsfoot.)

DP: But isn't "messages from the gods" the language of poetry?

NOB: (Stops, puts his hand on DP's shoulder and smiles in his most condescending and fatherly way) Yes, if you are a *conservative* poet.

(Many thoughts follow, as we walk on ... Charles Olson? How do the language poets fit in? Zukofsky? Cage, maybe. But I'm not a stranger there.)

DP: God, will I ever be able to wash the stink of Romanticism from me?

NOB: Interesting you call it Romanticism. But stink is right. If you watched as much MTV as I do, you'd be bored with love too.

(I had to smile. More walking. I showed Nobby how the willows were dioecious, either male or female.)

DP: There is a connection between Dionysus and Coyote.

NOB: Yes!

DP: There was a chief's daughter. A young warrior of good standing was courting her: he brought gifts of blankets, a horse, other things. He was doing it all correctly. Then one night Coyote slips in under the teepee flap and has sex with her.

[13] Algernon Charles Swinburne, "The Garden of Proserpine." Nobby seemed more obsessed with death than was usual, even for him.

[14] Cage (*John Cage, I-VI*, 444) defines love as "leaving space around the loved one." Brown found Cage's equation highly disturbing: it insisted on separation, which (by Freud) is death, not the union of love. Separation, that is, not being members of one body, is against Blake, Spinoza, and Ephesians V:30 ("Love Hath Reason"). Brown is suspicious that Cage doesn't mention death, and then, almost as an afterthought, adds that Spinoza didn't mention death either. Brown suspects that the problem may relate to the individual versus the species, and that the solution, if any, may relate to chance. The discussion remains unfinished.

NOB: (Stops, eyeball to eyeball) How do you think the women feel about Coyote?

DP: (Meets his gaze) I think they like him.

(Some silence. Then more walking, more talk on love and death. Anxiety. Pentheus. Pan. NOB stops, turns, quotes Swinburne, slowly and emphatically.)

NOB:

> *From too much love of living,*
> *From hope and fear set free,*
> *We thank with brief thanksgiving*
> *Whatever gods may be*
> *That no life lives for ever;*
> *That dead men rise up never;*
> *That even the weariest river*
> *Winds somewhere safe to sea.*[13]

(But we kept returning to love. I couldn't let it go.)

NOB: I'm bothered that love appears in the last sentence of *Finnegans Wake*: "A way a lone a last a loved a long the." If Joyce couldn't solve it, who can? Not John Cage! Love is all a mix up of language.[14]

DP: You don't think there is love without language?

NOB: (Thoughtful) No.

DP: I don't agree. I've seen elephants supporting a mate. I've seen lions get crazy and act funny. Wolves can get sheepish. And they mate for life.

NOB: That's just habit.

DP: Then we can adopt that cloak of glamour as our habit.

NOB: That's good. Is that yours?

DP: Yes ... With some help from KH. I might have said "grammar." Same root.

NOB: I KNOW the root. Who is KH?

[15] He hadn't lost any of his nastiness.

[16] (2007): Some days I think I may have been overly optimistic.

DP: A Goddess.

NOB: Another of those Sonoma witches you spoke of? Do they all read some witch's Bible?[15]

DP: No. And please do not misunderstand me. I use "witch" only in its broadest and most metaphorical sense. If I may be vulgarly generalizing, as the Santa Cruz women are into politics, the Sonoma women are into ... telepathy. And I find that very exciting.

(We stopped and sat on a log by the creek and a small falls.)

NOB: (Sighs) Yes, I would too. Fortunately, I'm too old.

DP: Then I should proceed?

NOB: Yes. Do you think they have a solution? I think the human race is doomed.

DP: She knows enough to have me interested. And I'm not a complete schmuck.[16]

NOB: No. But if only I could have trained you!

DP: You mean instead of this waste?

NOB: Yes, all that brilliancy, scattered and wasted. Drugs.

DP: See, Montaigne never worried about love. If he got horny, he just got laid. It was like eating breakfast.

NOB: Yes. That perks my interest in him.

DP: To be initiated into the women's circles, I may have to wear a dress. Duncan always stressed cross-dressing as part of shamanism.

NOB: Duncan was a narcissist. Put a page of Duncan alongside Spicer.

(We had reached the extremity of our walk. We found a log and sat down to rest.)

NOB: What are you writing now?

[17] Tom Marshall comments: "This is the opposite of my impression: I saw him longing for God."

DP: "Somewhere there be women who love Fools."

NOB: You were much influenced by Christianity.

DP: Yes.

NOB: That's why I can talk to you.

DP: Sooner or later, it all comes down to theology.

NOB: That's right! I'm trying to get rid of Christ.

DP: Me too.

NOB: Then you will continue my work after I am gone.

DP: *(Thinking this is a rather chancy proposition)*

NOB: I am embracing atheism. Maybe even Dionysus is too much.[17]

DP: I congratulate you, on your conversion.

NOB: It means there is a mistake in my books.

DP: Yes.

NOB: There is not much I can do about it now.

DP: I promise to steal, twist, warp, and otherwise generally corrupt all of your ideas that I can.

NOB: (Purses his lips)

DP: If this atheism of yours can't produce, maybe it is also a mistake.

(Walking in silence.)

NOB: It comes down to a wager.

DP: I think that may be the one point on which we are in agreement.

NOB: What is the alternative?

DP: Hmm. Let's see, is it really true? Is it really, really true? Is it really, really, really true? It won't do. Something must be risked.

[18] Lear, to Albany.

[19] *Love comes empty-handed; the eternal proletariat; like Cordelia, bringing Nothing.* (NOB, "A Reply to Herbert Marcuse," published in *Commentary*, March 1967)

[20] In *Closing Time*, Nobby equates "return to divination" with "a return to the language of the gods."

> *The original language is the language of the gods*
> *the language of the gods is mute speech ...*
> *The language of the gods is not spoken words but signs.*
> (CT 94-95)

And in *Love's Body*:

> *to transcend the antimony of sense and nonsense ... a victory over the reality principle; a victory for the god Dionysus; playing with fire, or madness; or speaking with tongues; the dialect of God is solecism.* (LB 258)

David Greenham (*The Resurrection of the Body*, 167) notes that in Vico's fifth age (the age of irony, our present age), "to await the return of the gods" is to witness the "return of barbarism." Nobby liked to quote Engels: "Only barbarians are capable of rejuvenating a world laboring under the death throes of unnerved civilization." Dionysus, of course, is the barbarian (as is, I might add, Bodhidharma).

NOB: Yes.

DP: And I'm too old for small bets. Besides, what do I have to lose?

NOB: (Stops, in DP's face) You have everything to lose.

DP: (Back in his face) Then so be it.

NOB: Oh, I'm just sorry I won't be around to see how it comes out.

DP: "It may be so, my lord."[18]

NOB: You like Lear. Not for me.

DP: Hah! No, not for you. You only closed your answer to Marcuse by saying that, like Cordelia, you bring nothing.[19]

NOB: (Has to smile)

DP: We're close to something here. A wager on the language of poetry.

NOB: I think the true language of poetry is gibberish.

(I was thinking of NOB's emphasis on farce, and gibberish as Pentecost, the tongue on fire.)[20]

DP: That one not begin believing one's own metaphors, and thereby court disaster.

NOB: That you stop taking yourself so seriously!

(We walked the last quarter mile in silence. On the drive back we tried to sum up some of the threads. Discussion of Blake led to the poet Clayton Eshleman: "A big Blake man," Nobby said.

Back at the Brown's driveway I put the car in neutral but left the engine running.)

NOB: Karl Schorske is going to visit me. How do you relate to academia?

DP: I have no relationship to academia whatsoever.

[21] And yet the earth moves, and a large interdisciplinary class at the University of California is currently using *Pharmako/Poeia* and *Pharmako/Dynamis* as required texts.

NOB: I don't think that is true. And they do confer a stamp of approval.

DP: I'm not anti. But Nobby, it would take a revolution like the sixties to bring my books into academia.[21]

NOB: You are a complete product of the sixties. Is there anything I can do to help you with your career?

DP: I wish there were.

NOB: It's been a lovely walk. Come back.

•

Over a year passed before I got back to Santa Cruz. I was shocked at Nobby's decline. I didn't think I could safely take him out for a walk. Beth didn't think so either, so we sat on the couch in the Brown's living room. I asked Nobby how he was doing and he answered matter-of-factly, "I'm failing." That may have been his longest complete sentence. I tried to maintain our rule of "no quarter" and challenged him to show what kind of philosopher he was. Nobby understood completely, but was unable to articulate an answer.

At times Nobby would stand up and pace a couple of nervous circles around the room, and then sit down again. Small talk only seemed to confuse him: he would look frightened or confused and start to get up again. He couldn't figure out what to do with his hands.

I noticed that I had begun to speak to him as one does to a child, and decided to read him my "Language of Birds." Nobby immediately settled and listened intently. I could see his mind following the twists and plays of the poem. Sometimes his excitement would bubble over and he would try to make a comment. In each case, however, after several abortive starts, he would give up, shake his head, and just pat me on the back. He liked the piece. A line about "Freud the seer" dismissing accidents made him laugh heartily. Mostly we just beamed at each other or knocked shoulders or just sat there in the presence of the gathering silence.

The last time I saw Nobby he was in the Alzheimer's care unit at a quality nursing home in Santa Cruz. He was sitting at a table with six other men and women, eating. There was no talking. Those who could feed themselves did so; a nurse would occasionally spoon-feed those who could not. Consciousness here was dim, they were caught up in an inexorable regression back to infancy, and then to death. But with whatever traces of volition and control they possessed, each of them worked to maintain dignity and decorum, a statement of the tragic nobility of the human spirit— the reason, I suppose, that men will walk to their own executions, rather than be dragged.

It took Nobby a long time to recognize me. I had just shaved off my beard for the first time in my adult life, and it had fooled even my father. Nobby suddenly grabbed my face, stroking my naked chin and beaming.

I asked him if things were as bad as they appeared. Nobby held my gaze for a long while and answered by returning to the demanding task of eating, of bringing a fork of food from the plate to his mouth without spilling.

Nobby died October 2, 2002.

•

> *Ama et fac quod vis.*
> —Augustine

> "Love and do what you wish!"
> —My last letter from N.O.B.

March 1997

APPENDIX 1
"FROM POLITICS TO METAPOLITICS"

Frederick William Atherton lecture
Harvard University, March 20, 1967
Norman O. Brown

My first response to the invitation of this honorable company
and to the wishes of Frederick William Atherton
"a topic related to ethical or social criticism"
was that it would be a pleasure to present my kind of
radicalism in this environment—
Since then I have been wondering about radicalism
and wondering about myself
These are times of great uncertainty and doubt as well as anguish.

Starting out in the Thirties
When to be young was to be a Marxist
I ask myself
What has happened since then?
What have I learned in my bizarre psychedelic trips
        I mean my books
What news is there that might be useful to the citizens
        the young citizens
        who are starting out now?
You have a right to ask how much, or how little.

So much has changed
perhaps the message is instability
permanent instability in the mind
corresponding to the permanent revolution in things
instability to be accepted as an eternal truth
like Heraclitean flux—

But in this Heraclitean flux, or fire,
there is for me also a Heraclitean Logos
the logos, the word, is One, or oneness
        unity
        unification
        the unification of the human race.

Intellectuals: for me the word still spells a vocation—
intellectuals who have been entrusted with the word, the Logos,
are called to work for unity.
If, as Blake said, the Fall is into Division
the vocation of the intellectual is to overcome the consequences
of the Fall.

I don't know about the proletariat, but
the intellectual, as such, has no fatherland—
or, to use another metaphor,
there is a heavenly city.

Logos seeks unification; and the fact it faces is Division
Alienation, in the old Marxist vocabulary
the rents, the splits, in the newer Freudian vocabulary
the schisms
the schizophrenia.

Now—if I may make a Great Leap Forward—
alienation is schizophrenia
the outcome of the collision between Marx and Freud is
their unification
the perception of the analogy between the two
the analogy between social and psychic
   society and soul
   body and body politic.

In the mythology of Marxism, the revolution is from below:
Those lower classes, lower depths, are the depths of
depth psychology
an underworld repressed by the bourgeois ego
a cauldron of energy and violence with the lid on
an anonymous mass, or social id—

If you take the psychoanalytical idea of projection seriously
the proletariat (if and when we perceive one) is us projected
   a collective projection
   a collective dream, or nightmare
   (the dream is in the language
   (and the language is acted upon
   (saying makes it so)

If you take the psychoanalytical idea of projection seriously
the ego constructs itself by projecting the other
the ego constructs itself by drawing an imaginary line
   between inside and outside
an imaginary boundary-line

And this imaginary boundary-line is the reality-principle
The reality-principle is the distinction between inner world and
external reality
and it is a false distinction.

"The false reality-principle"
This is to take psychoanalysis more seriously than the
psychoanalysts do
or to pass beyond psychoanalysis
Beyond the reality-principle is poetry
        taking metaphors seriously
        (metaphors and analogies)
        that way madness lies.

The disintegration of the boundary-line between inner and outer
        self and other
is the disintegration of the ego
the disintegration of the ego of the ego-psychologists
in Marxist terms, the disintegration of the bourgeois ego
        of bourgeois individualism
or alienation overcome—
The split between inside and outside is the primal split
        is the origin of alienation.

Already in Marxism
    the intellectual was to go to the masses
    bourgeois individualism, the separate self, was
    to be drowned in the proletarian ocean
Marxist thought substitutes for the reality of individuals the
reality of classes
But classes, as external realities, mutually external, are
not real either
it all really takes place in one body.

Marx, who, like Freud, is a genius who surpasses his own
limitations once said:
"the head of this emancipation is philosophy, its heart
the proletariat."
He means ego and id. Of course proletariat, if you
look at the word, must also be genital.

At any rate, it all takes place in one body
one body that has been mysteriously dismembered
    and needs to be remembered
to knit again these broken limbs into one body.
It must be some kind of embrace
    overcoming alienation.
Emerson used to say, There is only one Man
After Emerson, what happened, on the American continent,
to this intuition?

To perceive that it all really takes place in one body
is to transvalue the old political categories
to pass from politics to metapolitics
    or poetry.

The proletariat is dead
    but the proletariat is us
    long live the proletariat.
There is an inner Bastille to be captured
    to release the prisoners
or rather, the inner and the outer Bastille is the same Bastille
or rather, the distinction between inner and outer is the Bastille
    the false reality-principle
    the government of the reality-principle,
    to be overthrown
and the revolution is a visionary breakthrough
    or poetry
    or madness.
Revolution really is madness
    political revolutions
The French Revolution, the Russian Revolution
    Ten Days that Shook the World
    The Great Cultural Revolution
All the pathology of the twentieth century
The madness of the millennia breaking out
    as Nietzsche prophesied—
The problem really is madness
There is a point where Marat and de Sade are one.

What to do with madness
The political solution to the problem of madness is
              divide and conquer
              segregation and repression
              (like in asylums)
              perpetual conflict
the political revolution is a temporary break-down followed by the reinstitution of repression
a cycle of explosion and repression
        activity and passivity
               in eternal recurrence
Perpetual conflict is the rule of politics
        the reality-principle
        the world as we know it
Is there any alternative?

A metapolitical solution to the problem of madness
would see politics as madness
and madness as the solution to politics.
Breaking down the boundaries is breaking down the reality-principle
unification lies beyond the reality-principle
the communion is Dionysian.

Madness is even the solution to the problem of madness
        it is sanity that needs to be saved
              (I don't mean, save your sanity)
it was the greatness of Freud to see through, to bore through, the wall
        separating sanity and insanity
it is all a problem of communication
the poet says, Madness is oneness lost
But oneness regained is madness also.

Can we liberate instead of repress
Can we find a way of being permanently unstable—
Emerson says: "Whenever man comes, there comes revolution"
              there is that great flame
It is the idea of permanent revolution
But permanent revolution cannot be political revolution
      permanent political revolution is fratricide, or suicide,

      it is the situation we are in now
         it is the situation we are trying to escape from

To save the revolution it must be given a metapolitical meaning
         as madness, or poetry
         uninterrupted poetry:
         surrealism, to stamp out reality.

Madness and Civilization
      a very serious question
Here I differ from one of your sages
      B. F. Skinner, *Walden Two* (202): "Nothing
      comes from general frothing at the mouth"
         I have done some frothing in my time

Madness is an eternal truth
and some shaking or quaking is testimony to the need
for liberation
      to the uncomfortableness of culture
It is possible that the future is a contented humanity
      without neurotics like me
but I don't think so
      I don't think the future is behavioral engineering
         getting rid of unhappiness, maladjustment, madness
My utopia is
      an environment that works so well
      that we can run wild in it
      anarchy in an environment that works
the environment works, does all the work
      a fully automatic environment
      all public utilities
      or communication-networks
(the engineering contribution to unification; unification is also a matter of engineering)
My teachers in utopian engineering are John Cage and Buckminster Fuller
but wasn't there a divinely absurd anticipation in Marx, or Engels, saying that the government of persons will be replaced by the administration of things—
The environment can do all the work

Serious thought, thought as work, in pursuit of *Wirklichkeit*,
is about over
Wirklichkeit, the German word for reality, the reality-principle

The reality-principle is about over

Thought as work can be buried in machines and computers
the work left to be done is to bury thought; quite a job

To put thought underground
    as communication-network, sewage system, power lines
So that wildness can come above ground
Technological rationality can be put to sleep
so that something else can awaken in the human mind
something like the god Dionysus
something which cannot be programmed.

The ordering of the physical environment will release
unparalleled
quantities and forms of human disorder

The future, if there is one, is machines and madness
    What men or gods are these? What maidens both?
    What mad pursuit? What struggle to escape?

The struggle should not be, is no longer, really, the struggle
for existence.

But unification is not only a matter of engineering.
Marshall McLuhan is taken by some to mean that technology is
bringing us into a global village
Buckminster Fuller is taken by some to mean that technology is
bringing us a global network of public services
But there is some obstruction
There is some obstacle impeding the free flow of unification

        political divisions, boundaries
        but, at a deeper level, the reality-principle
        the boundary between Self and Other
        the logic which divides

                    which most people think is reason itself or rationality
Rationality and the reality-principle are obstacles to unification.

But fortunately there is a disturbance in the house of reason

Ever since the age of reason something like a collective
break-down
    has been taking place
    a destruction of reason
    a destruction in which intellect must immerse

In order that the disintegration of the ego may be the birth
of some
kind of collective consciousness
In order that the logic of division may give way to the logos
of union
The logos of union whose name is, or one of whose
names is, ever since the time of Hegel,
        dialectics.

We are still Hegel's contemporaries
    even in America, as Emerson knew
    living in the last days, the end of history
    the age of revolution and apocalypse

And therefore in that No Man's Land between reason
and madness
        which is dialectics
      Reason and Revolution is really Reason and Madness
Dialectics is the revolt against rationalism
the discovery that self contradiction is the essence of reality
the opening to the absurd

Dialectics is intellect seeking union with energy
    in Marx, philosophy seeking union with the proletariat
    in Freud, ego seeking union with id

In dialectics nothing is stable, movement is all
    a logic of passion

Mandelstam in Russia in 1921 (Mandelstam, not
Lenin; a poet not a politician): "a new heroic era
has opened in the life of the word. The word is flesh
and bread. It shares the fate of bread and flesh:
suffering."

Dialectics is a dialectic of life against death
    death is a part of life
like Freud, Hegel says the goal of all life is death;
    "The nature of the finite lies in this, that it dissolves itself"
    it must go under
    this is self contradiction in practice, in action—

Hegel, *Phenomenology*: "Not the life that shrinks from death and keeps itself
undefiled by devastation (*Verwüstung*), but the life that suffers death
and preserves itself in death is the life of the Spirit. Spirit gains its truth
by finding itself in absolute dismemberment. (*Zerrissenheit*)."

Dismemberment, absolute dismemberment
the Spirit is Dionysus, the god who is dismembered
Dionysus, or schizophrenia
schizophrenia is spirit in absolute dismemberment
        déchirement ontologique
Dionysus is also union, communion

Dialectics is the dissolution of all partial statements till they are
lost in the whole
    "the truth is in the whole"

And the union or communion is madness
dialectic is drunkenness or dancing
the Bacchanalian revel of the categories in which not one
member is sober.

Hegel nevertheless made a Hegelian system
and Marx also made a system
and so did Freud; at least the Freud whom the Psychoanalytical
Associations worship

Systems, Marxist, Freudian, can be, as they say, flexible
But flexibility is not enough—
Mind, or spirit, or life, must learn how to die
        it must go under

All these systems have immortal longings on them
        that is why they are dead
        born dead
        representing from the hour of the birth the dead hand
        of the past

The flexibility is wriggling to avoid death
what they mean by rationality is, don't die
        be consistent—
The rule of die-in-order-to-live
    diese Stirb' und Werde
is not flexibility but metamorphosis
is not political but poetical.

The real action in *Love's Body*
        (you can tell by the creaking)
        is to find an alternative to systematic form
Dialectics, in flight from the systematic, finds refuge in
aphoristic form

Aphorism: the word smells of literary self-consciousness
the reality is brokenness
        words in absolute dismemberment
        or even, absolute self-contradiction.

We have been told that the medium is the message
Aphoristic form has political or rather metapolitical implications—
Politics is systems
There is a hidden truth or secret
        that is what the Unconscious is all about
But it cannot be put into systematic, reified, permanent form
Systematic reified permanent form creates an elite who possess
the secret
        (Platonic academy, occult order, political party,
            the repository of the secret)

Mass mysticism is poetry
        an open secret—
"The truth is in the whole"

But the whole is in any part, not in the system—
        infinity in a grain
        and in an instant
        the whole is here or nowhere

Aphorism is instant dialectic
        the instantaneous flip instead of the elaborate system
Only so do we have a form of intellect that is so easy
        that any child could do it
        or, only a child can do it
And so perishable
        that it cannot be hoarded by any elite
        or stored in any institution
A form of dialectics, therefore, unequivocally on the side
of freedom
        or madness.

And finally
        (using Hegel again as my landmark)
The Hegelian dialectic is the simultaneous total affirmation of this
world and its total negation
Both the right-wing Hegelians and the left-wing Hegelians are in it
Both the Marxian change the world and the Nietzschean
everything always the same
The hard thing here is the Nietzschean affirmation—

Nietzsche says
        "He does not negate any more"
At any rate intellectuals should watch their language
The critical judgement
        which separates the sheep from the goats
                We and They
critical judgement is party or sect formation
        is scission of the one body
        and projection of part of ourselves
Intellect as protest

           or great refusal (Hawthorn-Melville's No in Thunder)
       gets us nowhere
in this mess, rectitude or righteousness is unobtainable
                and will not save us.

What kind of language might be helpful?
        Instead of morality, metaphor
                to ferry us across
                the language which unifies
        The language of healing, or making whole is not
                psychoanalysis, but poetry.

Poetry is the visionary form, or explosion
        which overthrows the reality-principle
        and transforms this world, just the way it is,
                without changing a thing
                the transformation is the unification.

These are the fragmentary moments which bring something new
into the world
Fragmentary moments: there isn't anything we can count on
or accumulate.

Poetry is the solvent which dissolves
            the rigorous stereotypes of political ideology
            the numb automatism of political reflexes
            the somnambulist gravity of literal believers
These are the obstructions to be dissolved
                to be loosened up—
Poetry is the transforming spirit of play
                metaphorical play

Begin today
        no place needs the transforming spirit of play more than
        the University
        that Bastille of literalism
        especially that Bastille inside the Bastille in which I live,
        the Humanities

Appendix 1   213

The great revolutionary intellectual of the 20th century:
James Joyce
>	who reduced all that solemn nonsense to nonsense
>	leading us in the path to which Wittgenstein directed us
>	from disguised nonsense to patent nonsense
>	a transition that is accomplished not by linguistic
>	analysis but by poetry.

The primal Logos is the poetic Logos
and the Logos of unification is poetry

The intellectual, to whom was entrusted the word, was given
the power to unify the world this way

There are also engineers, to whom is given the power to unify the world in another way

There are also politicians.
It is the tale of Shem and Shaun
>	who turn into Shem, Ham, and Japheth
>>	or Tom, Dick, and Harry.

APPENDIX 2
"LOVE HATH REASON, REASON NONE"

*A lecture given at Boston University, December 15, 1993
Boston Colloquium for the Philosophy of Science
in honor of Professor Robert S. Cohen
Norman O. Brown*

Bob Cohen will allow me to begin by remembering a fellow traveller with a very good libido, Herbert Marcuse.

What would Herbert Marcuse say today, in 1993? What would Herbert Marcuse have thought about *die Wende*, the term used in East Germany to refer to the events between October 1989 and Spring 1990? *Die Wende*: wending or winding: a turn, or trope. I found the term in Peter Marcuse, *Missing Marx*, "a personal and political journal of a year in East Germany, 1989-1990." *Missing Marx*—Peter Marcuse spells it MARX: the pun is deliberate: the cover reproduces a 100 mark note of the German Democratic Republic, 1975, with a grand picture of Karl Marx.

Missing Marx. I am still arguing with Herbert Marcuse, over the word "love." "Love Mystified: A Critique of Norman O. Brown," by Herbert Marcuse, *Commentary*, February 1967 (reprinted in Herbert Marcuse, *Negations*). What, if anything, is wrong with Karl Marx? We are asking the question again in 1993. And answering it: "Love hath reason, reason none."

"Love Mystified: A Critique of Norman O. Brown" by Herbert Marcuse was a critique of *Love's Body*. Marcuse was right: *Love's Body* is too Christian; Marcuse was right about the confusion of Christ with Dionysus. There is a Dionysian Christianity—how else are we to understand Blake? But the time has come to differentiate Dionysus from Christ. *Tempora mutantu,. nos et mutamur in illis.* The times they are a-changing; we must change with them.

It is time for recantation, or at least reconsideration, of *Love's Body*. Ch. IV, "Unity." The romance of "Unity." The Christian roots (St. Paul)—"we are all members of one body"—transfigured, made new, by Blake; made "scientific" or "materialistic" by Spinoza; made political by Marxism—"Workers of the world, unite"; the Communist Internatlonale "shall be the human race." The energy of *Love's Body*, Ch. IV, is from this concoction: all this discovered to be the true meaning of psychoanalysis.

It is true that there is a different tone to other parts of *Love's Body*: Ch. XI, "Fraction." Reality is not a seamless unity: Yeats is quoted saying:

> Nothing can be sole or whole
> That has not been rent.

A note of masochism as well as pluralism is sounded: "to be is to be vulnerable."

Can we go forward with Dionysus; with the notion of chance; against Marxist determinism; against Freudian determinism? Determinism implies coherence; coherence implies unity. Chance introduces incoherence; chance implies autonomy of parts: Spinoza can't be right. The idea of chance breaks the Christian synthesis and opens up the Dionysian future. Chance disunites; loosens the fabric of the world; introduces an irrational swerve. Chance disunites and so does death. The individual is not the same as the species.

Differentiating Dionysus from Christ—the parting of the ways is already in *Love's Body*, Ch. X, "Fire"; written in the weekend of the Cuban missile crisis, when the Fire next Time seemed about to fall this time.

> *Love is all fire; and so heaven and hell are the same place. As in Augustine, the torments of the damned are part of the felicity of the redeemed. Two cities; which are one city. Eden is a fiery city; just like hell.*
> Cf. Augustine, *De Civitate Dei*, XXII, 30.

This passage in *Love's Body* names the principle of love, and makes it the reason for rejecting Christianity; or, at least, for rejecting Augustine; or, at least, for rejecting Augustine's City of God with its vision of the redeemed as distinct and separate from the damned, Heaven distinct from Hell, Inferno distinct and separate from Paradiso; as even in Dante. Augustine does entertain the objection that the happiness of the saints in heaven, which has to be unalloyed, will be spoilt by the thought of the others—mothers, fathers, sisters, brothers, lovers—being tortured in Hell. Augustine, no man to flee from paradox, answers that the saints in Heaven will enjoy the torments of the wicked in Hell, because of course they love justice.

In this passage of *Love's Body*, Christianity—Augustine—is rejected in the name of love, "To go beyond all Christianity with hyper-Christianity, and not to remain satisfied with merely throwing it out." Nietzsche speaking. What is being rejected is the notion of eternal damnation. What is being rejected is the Augustinian synthesis of love and justice. Hyper-Christian is to embrace love and reject justice.

Jesus said "Judge not, that ye be not judged." Christian civilization never found a way to put that into practice. Jesus also authorized horrendous apocalyptic pictures of the Last Judgment: when sheep will be separated from goats; and some will be cast into outer darkness, and there will be weeping and wailing and gnashing of teeth. The apocalyptic imagination—Jesus had it; I have had it too. Marxism has it: "'tis the final conflict." John Paul II too: "the prospect of eternal damnation must be held out as the ultimate sanction."

Missing Marx. The Marxist allegiance to justice: I remember Karl Marx's scorn for Utopian Socialists who talk about love. I remember, from my youth in the 1930s, "Justice thunders condemnation" in the Communist Internationale. *Das Kapital* is a plea for justice against exploitation; exploitation is the extraction of surplus (unjust) value. Marx is the last of the mediaeval schoolmen, looking for the just price.

The Buddhists have reincarnation in order to be able to say there is justice: the cause was in a previous incarnation. Plato in the *Republic* invents the myth of Er to show that God is just: the souls, before reincarnation, chose their future lot or life. The individual has chosen; the blame is his; God is blameless. The contradiction between love and justice. I don't know if the divine Plato lost his way here, or stumbled elsewhere out of philosophy into poetry. The *Republic* is about justice; but the *Phaedrus* is a palinode celebrating love as Dionysian madness, and the *Symposium* celebrates love as Dionysian intoxication.

From Anaximander to Rawls, justice is rationality: "there must be a reason." But love hath reason, reason none. Let us dump justice, together with causality. Too long the world has been a mad-house.

Anaximander said, "according to the ordering of time." I need a new sense of time, a new sense of newness. Even in 1990, the title *Apocalypse and/or Metamorphosis* is stuck in a rut. As if our choice still were between Hebraism (Apocalypse) and Hellenism (Metamorphosis).

The trouble with Apocalypse—the trouble with America—it expects a new age. A new age now begins: *novus ordo saeclorum.* It is too Christian. It was a wonderful thing to break the classical wheel of eternal recurrence with the Christian separation of B.C. from A.D. A voice from heaven came saying "Behold, I make all things new"; *Apocalypse of St. John the Divine*, XXI:5. The Idea of Revolution: the apocalyptic sense of newness in the Marxist mythology, so futuristic: "'Tis the final conflict"; tomorrow all will be utterly changed. Crowding all that need for newness into one apocalyptic moment.

Freud's Jewishness entered deeply into the structure of his ideas, from *Totem and Taboo* to *Moses and Monotheism*. There is really no new understanding of newness in Freud. It was not wrong, in 1966, to confront psychoanalysis with a Christian-Marxist demand for newness. *Love's Body* (p.266):

> Looking, therefore, upon sin, upon mortality, upon time flying by, upon moaning and labor and sweat, upon ages succeeding one another without rest, senselessly from infancy into old age—looking at these things, let us see in them the old man, the old day, the old song, the Old Testament. But if we turn to the things that are to be renewed, let us find a new man, a new day, a new song, the New Testament—and we shall love this newness so that we shall not fear there any oldness.

Augustine In Ladner, *The Idea of Reform*, pp.236-237.

The power of Augustinian Christianity. It will not easily be superseded. I need a post-Christian understanding of newness; a post-Christian understanding of time.

The apocalyptic sense of newness, whether in Marxism or in *Love's Body*, is too Christian. Marcuse is right: Ch. XII of *Love's Body*, "Resurrection," is too Christian. (I hesitated whether to call Ch. XII "Resurrection" or "Revolution.") The energy in Ch. XII of *Love's Body* is to effect a marriage between psychoanalysis and a Christian sense of time: to demand from psychoanalysis a Christian sense of renewal. Archetypal patterns of eternal recurrence discovered in psychoanalysis are identified with theological patterns of redemptive history (Christ as the second Adam, etc.). By this path the conclusion is reached that "There is another kind of Protestantism possible, a Dionysian Christianity"—the final destination to which Marcuse objected.

The confusion in *Love's Body* reflects the confusion in the American counter-culture of the period. "Dionysian Christianity" seems to be a kind of ecstatic disaffiliation to be achieved by extraordinary feats of vision—a "miraculous pregnancy"—"symbolic consciousness." "Symbolic consciousness" seems to be an awareness of "eternity" (as in Blake), identified with "eternal recurrence" (as in Nietzsche), and with the repetition-compulsion (as in Freud). It is only in the most recent period of history—after *die Wende* of 1989—that I begin to see in the idea of chance the Dionysian alternative. The idea of chance, so much identified with John Cage; my friend since 1960; but I would not listen. I was a determinist; first a Marxist determinist; then Freudian determinist. The world of chance; the world of chance mutations. In *Love's Body*, Ch. XII, it says "Nothing happens for the first time." That is dead wrong: everything happens for the first time. That is the meaning of chance; it contradicts both the Christian idea of eternity and the Nietzschean idea of eternal recurrence.

"If there is no risk there is no future" (Michael Milken in *New York Times*, 10/16/93). If there is no future, there is no time. If there is no risk, there is no death, no self-destruction. Jesus on the other hand said "Lead us not into temptation." What on earth did Jesus mean? Teaching us to pray to our Father which art in Heaven; asking Him not to lead us into temptation; as if our Father might be the Tempter; or tempted to be the Tempter. Does "temptation" mean "risk"? The Greek word is *peirasmos*: the same root as in our word "empirical," meaning "attempt," or "try," or "experiment." Lead us not into experimentation. Don't gamble; stay away from Las Vegas. Einstein said God does not gamble; so much the worse for the idea of God. Maybe God is an old Devil: more like Dionysus.

Mysterium Amoris. It sounds ridiculous in English: two words too often profaned. John Cage, in *Themes and Variations* (1982), repeated in his Harvard lectures (1990), offers a mysterious definition of love. "Love = leaving space around the loved one." Love = resisting the urge to unite, out of consideration for the loved one, whom it threatens to destroy?? "Love = leaving space around the loved one." Overcoming the temptation not to take John Cage seriously—his definition emphasizes the separateness of the beloved. Separation = death, Eros = union, says Freud. We are dealing with the principle of individuation. Cage's definition insists on separation. It is a way of separating himself from the emphasis on love as union, or unity; as in *Love's Body*. We are not members of one body, in spite of Ephesians V:30, and Blake, and Spinoza. There is some mystery here: something to do with death—although John Cage does not mention it—death as well as love: Freud's Thanatos or *Todestrieb*; something to do with the *principium individuationis*, the relation of the individual to the species.

Americans think of individuals—individual persons—as real, as having substantial reality. Spinoza is the inevitable opposite of American individualism and pluralism: individuals are only modes in the one substance, God or Nature. Spinoza took no account of death. *Love's Body* envisages Dionysus as a mystical sense able to arrive at that unity that was the goal of Spinozistic rationalism: "Dionysus, the mad god, breaks down the boundaries; releases the prisoners; abolishes repression; and abolishes the *principium individuatlonis*, substituting for it the unity of man and the unity of man with nature" (p.161). But death cannot be drowned in oceanic feelings.

Mysterium Amoris. Plato's *Symposium*. Not Diotima's exposition of Platonic philosophy, but Aristophanes' poetic myth of the incompleteness of the sexually differentiated individual (the principle of individuation). The sexes are sections, formed by bisection of a more complete being. "Each one of us is therefore the symbol of a human being"—*anthropou sumbolon*—not a human being but the symbol of a human being. Aristophanes' myth interprets symbolism as the sign of Paradise Lost: the loss of a previous condition of unity which it is the (futile) aim of love to recover. Freud says the same thing in *The Interpretation of Dreams*: "The symbolic relation seems to be a remainder and a reminder of a former identity." The desire and pursuit of the whole.

The metaphysical (metapsychological) implications of psychoanalysis are cautiously explored by Freud in *Beyond the Pleasure-Principle,* and incautiously elaborated in that neglected masterpiece by the beloved disciple Sandor Ferenczi: *Thalassa: A Theory of Genitality*. Biological evolution is the result of a sequence of catastrophes, beginning with the great catastrophe which split organic from inorganic matter, and which bequeathed to all forms of life the "thalassal regressive tread." The goal of all life is death; to return to the condition of lifeless (inorganic) matter out of which life came: "to nullify the process of being born."

Psychoanalysis ends up with the tragic wisdom of Silenus—the point of view Nietzsche wrestled with in the *Birth of Tragedy*—"Oh, wretched ephemeral race; why do you compel me to tell you what it were most expedient for you not to hear? What is best of all is beyond your reach forever: not to be born, not to be, to be nothing."

The psychoanalytical movement initiated by Freud ends up with the supremacy of death. This outcome seems almost predetermined by the matrix of nineteenth century science in which psychoanalysis was born. Does the idea of chance open up a way out or a way forward?

Each of us is not a human being, but only the symbol of a human being. We are not individuals; we are pieces—tesserae, tokens, or tallies—temporary repositories of value in a game of chance. Paraphrasing Lucretius: the life that mortals live is not their private property: it is more like a torch transmitted in a relay race. It is a game of chance: *le jeu de l'amour et du hazard*; the dicing table of the gods.

What was Freud trying to say at the end of *Civilization and Its Discontents*—

> Men have brought their powers of subduing the forces of nature to such a pitch that by using them they could now very easily exterminate one another to the last man. They know this—hence arises a great part of the current unrest, their dejection, their mood of apprehension. And now it may be expected that the other of the two "heavenly forces," eternal Eros, will put forth his strength so as to maintain himself alongside of his equally immortal adversary. But who can foresee the outcome? Aber wer kann den Erfolg und Ausgang voraussehen?

What was Nietzsche trying to say in the paragraph titled "End" in his notebooks—

> We Europeans have within us the blood of those who died for their faith; we've taken morality terribly seriously; there is nothing we haven't sacrificed for it. On the other hand, our intellectual refinement is due principally to a vivisection of our conscience. We still don't know where we'll have to go leaving this ancient territory. But this soil, having communicated a strength to us, now aimlessly pushes us toward shoreless climes that remain as yet unexploited and undiscovered; we have no choice, and we're forced [to] be conquerors

because we no longer have a country we want to remain in. A secret confidence impels us, confidence stronger than our negations. Our very strength doesn't allow us to stay on this ancient soil; we'll take a chance, start risking ourselves; the world's still full of treasures, and it's better to perish than become weak and vicious. Our very vigor drives us to high seas where all suns until now have set: we know that there's a new world ...

Let us find a new man, a new day, a new song, a New Testament. Let us find a new understanding of newness; a new understanding of Love and Death.

THE GRAY LOVERS

When the two gray lovers
>shared their wine
with strangers, they did not know
>that their guests were gods

who would repay
>the gift of the fruits
of their long cultivated vineyards
>with a gift in turn.

When nubs of rootlets roughened
>the soles of their feet
and green buds and leaves
>sprouted from their arms and hands,

they hardly noticed—they
>could not have seen,
as the gods had seen so clearly,
>the forests and gardens

already grown up
>in the tangled years
between them, the gods,
>whose seeing goes beyond our own,

had simply given wine for wine
>and forest for forest,
returned richness where
>there was richness before,

and intoxication
>where there was already delight.
To deny the gifts of the gods
>would deny the scars and furrows

of your face, the forest,
>and a gnarled vineyard
so late in autumn
>still bearing fruit.

—Dale Pendell

NORMAN O. BROWN

1947 *Hermes the Thief,* University of Wisconsin

1948 Review of Jean Anouilh's *Antigone, The Wesleyan Argus,* v.81:35 pp.2

1949 "The Humanities at Wesleyan University," *The Humanities in General Education,* ed. Carl J. McGrath, Dubuque, Iowa, pp.30-41

1949 Review of W.H. Auden's *Portable Greek Reader, Classical Journal,* v.44, pp.433ff

1949 Review of M. J. Mellink's *Hyakinthos, American Journal of Archeology,* v.52, pp.218

1951 "Pindar, Sophocles, and the Thirty Years' Peace,"*Transactions and Proceedings of the American Philological Association,*v.82, pp.1-28

1952 "Pindar, Sophocles, and the Thirty Years' Peace," *Transactions of the American Philological Association,* v.82. pp.1-28

1952 "The Homeric Hymn to Hermes" (translation), in *Classics in Translation,* v.1: *Greek Literature,* ed. Paul MacKendrick and H. M. Howe, University of Wisconsin, pp.81-87

1953 "Greece—Ancient History and Culture: to 330 A.D.," *Encyclopedia Americana,* v.13, pp.374-389

1953 "Hermes," Ibid., v.14, pp.131-132

1953 "The Birth of Athena," *Transactions and Proceedings of the American Philological Association,* v.83, pp.130-143

1953 "The Homeric Hymn to Hennes" (translation), in *The Greek Poets,* ed. Moses Hadas, Modem Library, pp.130-135

1953 "The Arts of Love," *Wesleyan Cardinal,* Autumn 1952, pp.7-8, 24

1953 *Hesiod's Theogony* (translation, with an introduction by Brown), The Liberal Arts Press

1954 Review of A. J. Festugiere's *Personal Religion Among the Greeks, American Journal of Philology,* v.76, pp.435-437

A PARTIAL BIBLIOGRAPHY

1957 "Psychoanalysis and the Classics," *Classical Journal*, v.52, March 1957, pp.241-245

1959 *Life Against Death*, Wesleyan University Press, Middletown, Connecticut

1961 "Apocalypse: The Place of Mystery in the Life of the Mind," *Harper's Magazine*, v.222:1332, May 1961, pp.46-49

1963 "We Must Write A Letter to Robert Duncan," *Wesleyan Cardinal*, Autumn 1963

1966 *Love's Body*, Random House, New York

1967 "A Reply to Herbert Marcuse," *Commentary*, v.A3:3, March, pp.83-84

1967 "From Politics to Metapolitics," *Caterpillar* #1, v.1:1, Clayton Eshleman, ed., October, pp.62-94

1970 "Daphne, or Metamorphosis," *Myths, Dreams, and Religion*, Dutton & Co., New York, ed. Joseph Campbell, pp.91-110

1970 "A Homage to Propertius," *Caterpillar* #13, Clayton Eshleman, ed., October 1970

1971 *Book of Ours*, with Nor Hall (a class reader)

1972 "Metamorphoses II: Actaeon," *American Poetry Review*, v.1:1, November-December, pp.38-40

1973 "Rieff's 'Fellow Teachers,'" *Salmagundi*, no. 24, pp.34-45

1973 *Closing Time*. Random House, New York

1973 "Lupercalia," *New Literary History*, v.4, pp.541-556

1974 "Rome—A Psychoanalytical Study," *Arethusa*, v.7:1, pp.95-102

1976 "On Interpretation," *Evolution of Consciousness: Studies in Polarity*, Wesleyan University Press, pp.34-41

1981 "Universal History with Cosmopolitan Intent," *Democracy*, v.1:1, pp.80-92

1982 "Addenda on Ellul," *Democracy*, v.2:4, pp.119-126

1984 "The Apocalypse of Islam," *Social Text,* #8, Winter 1983/84, pp.155-170

1986 "Philosophy and Prophecy: Spinoza's Hermeneutics," *Political Theory,* v.14:2, May 1986, pp.195-214

1987 "Homage to Robert Duncan," *Sulfur* #19, Clayton Eshleman, ed., Spring 1987, pp.11-23

1987 "The Apocalypse of Islam," in *Facing Apocalypse,* V. Andrews, R. Bosnak, K. W. Goodwin (eds.), Spring Publications, Dallas, Texas, pp.137-162

1989 "Metamorphosis III, The Divine Narcissus," Sulfur #25, Clayton Eshleman, ed., pp.202-216

1989 "John Cage," in *John Cage at 75,* R. Fleming, W. Duckworth, eds., Bucknell Review, v.32, no.2, pp.97-118

1991 *Apocalypse and/or Metamorphosis,* University of California

1993 "Love Hath Reason, Reason None," lecture given at Boston University, publ. 2007, this volume

2005 "John Cage," *Aufgabe* #5, E. Tracy Grinnell, ed., pp.73-94

n.d. "Inauguration," unpublished ms.

ABOUT THE AUTHOR

Dale Pendell is the author of the award-winning *Pharmako* trilogy, a literary, shamanic, and pharmacological study of psychoactive plants. His poetry is widely anthologized, most recently in *The Wisdom Book of American Buddhist Poetry*. Besides writing, Dale has been a consultant for herbal product development and a computer scientist.

He and his wife Laura and a familiar cat live in the foothills of the Sierra in California, where they grow pine trees, oak trees, and manzanita. Their performance group, Oracular Madness, often appears at Burning Man.

AUTHOR'S ACKNOWLEDGEMENTS

I would like to thank the following people for their encouragement in completing this project: Jeremy Bigalke, Tom Brown, Scott Clements, Clayton Eshleman, Denis Kelly, Tom Marshall, Andrew Schelling, and, most especially, my wife and partner Laura Pendell.